THE VIRTUES

Ku czci

MAKSYMILIANA KOLBEGO

rycerza Niepokalanej

THE VIRTUES

THE STANTON LECTURES 1973–4

PETER GEACH

Professor of Logic, University of Leeds

CAMBRIDGE UNIVERSITY PRESS

CAMBRIDGE

LONDON · NEW YORK · MELBOURNE

Published by the Syndics of the Cambridge University Press
The Pitt Building, Trumpington Street, Cambridge CB2 IRP
Bentley House, 200 Euston Road, London NW1 2DB
32 East 57th Street, New York, NY 10022, USA
296 Beaconsfield Parade, Middle Park, Melbourne 3206,
Australia

First published 1977

Printed in Great Britain by
Western Printing Services Ltd, Bristol

Library of Congress Cataloguing in Publication Data
Geach, Peter Thomas
The Virtues
(The Stanton lectures; 1973-4)
1. Virtues–Addresses, essays, lectures
I. Title.   II. Series
BV4630.G4   241'.4   76-19628
ISBN 0 521 21350 9

ANALYTICAL TABLE OF CONTENTS

Analytical Table of Contents

Faith reveals what man's last end is; so those who lack faith cannot properly understand why faith is needed. Faith is God's gift; I try here only to remove obstacles to faith.   21

To show what saving faith is, we need to show what men are saved *for* and what they are saved *from*. What men are saved *for* is their chief end: to know and love God. But just as most acorns do not grow into oaks, although that is their end, so not all men realize their chief end: though an acorn that never becomes an oak, or a lost man, is not allowed to be useless.   21

Men achieve their end by free choice, and can miss it only by perverse free choice, since all men receive sufficient grace for their salvation. But the dark mystery of sin is not explained merely by the existence of free choice. A Christian will believe that sin is permitted only for the scope it gives to the redemptive love of Christ and his followers.   22

What men are saved *from* is sin; not only personal sin but Original Sin. In view of the corruption of the whole Adamic stock, only those who are individually given the new life of Christ can be saved, each for himself; there is corporate corruption, but not corporate salvation, of the human race. So to understand saving faith we must discuss Original Sin.   24

Chapter 3. Hope

Hope as a virtue makes sense on the view that man's last end is neither impossible of attainment, nor perfectly assured, for any given individual. The way to eternal life may be very arduous; and

There is dialogue between God and his rational creatures; they make known their petitions to God, and God declares his promises to them. Only Divine promises, by One whose rationality we share in, can warrant us in trusting that Nature will conform to our standards of rational expectation: this is a Jewish idea ('the covenant of day and night'). 53

God alone is immortal by nature; rational creatures exist for as long as he wills. But man's mind is not tied down to the practical matters of mortal life, and can desire the Eternal. Some philosophers have thought we should be content to have known that the Eternal exists and we have some share in its nature; this would leave little room for *hope*. Few men have claimed direct knowledge of the Eternal in this life; and most of such claims must be fraud or delusion. 55

Men really die; survival of a separated soul would not be survival of a man. Can we ask concerning a dead man what his soul is doing right *now*? There are reasons for doubting the common idea of continuous unilinear time. Even in this life successive thoughts are not simply correlatable with physical processes in their times of occurrence; and again there are well-known difficulties about assigning time to dreams. Moreover, alternative futures cannot be accommodated in a picture of unilinear time. So perhaps what the souls of the dead do between

Chapter 5. Prudence

Chapter 7. *Temperance*

PREFACE

The course of Stanton Lectures given in 1972–3 had the general topic 'Freedom and Prediction'. When I was preparing the three years' lecture notes for publication in the year 1974–5, for which the University of Leeds kindly gave me leave of absence, I found that they would need considerably more revision for this course than for the other two: I have therefore postponed publication of this course.

The present course of eight lectures on 'The Virtues' was delivered in Cambridge in 1973–4 and redelivered as the Hägerström Lectures at the University of Uppsala in April 1975. I thank my Swedish hosts for the honour they did me, for their hospitality, and for the many hours of peaceful solitude that gave me a much needed opportunity for important revisions. I fear Hägerström was then a mere name to me; what I have since read of him makes it apparent that a greater divergence of views and attitudes could scarcely be imagined than between him and this Hägerström Lecturer; I think, however, that my previous writings gave fair notice of what I was likely to say.

I am very grateful as before to the Master and Fellows of St John's College, Cambridge, for the hospitality they gave me, continued during the year's leave of absence from Leeds that I spent in Cambridge revising the work. *Finis coronat opus*.

P. T. GEACH

WHY MEN NEED THE VIRTUES

The definite article in my title is significant. I am concerned with why men need the seven virtues to which tradition gives pre-eminence: the theological virtues of faith, hope, and charity, and the cardinal virtues of prudence, temperance, justice, and courage. I commit myself to the thesis that all of these *are* virtues: and I shall argue that this thesis cannot rationally be doubted so far as the four cardinal virtues are concerned. That faith and hope, in the theological senses of the words, are virtues does of course depend on a contestable theological position; I shall not try to *demonstrate* that they are virtues needful to man, but only to make it clear what sort of disposition is ascribed to a man in saying he has faith or hope and to show what general view of man would warrant us in calling these virtues. I might find it easier to win assent to the thesis that charity or love is a virtue; but I could do so only by cheating, only by exploiting ambiguities. Both 'charity' and 'love' are words familiarly used for qualities very different from the theological virtue of charity – indeed they often signify qualities that in my book are not virtues at all.

For some time, for reasons I need not discuss, moral philosophers rather neglected the virtues; Philippa Foot has recently made what I take to be a move in the right direction by discussing the virtues rather than goodness

in general.[1] This move has naturally not met with general approval. Hare, for example, has protested that it is well 'to be suspicious, if any moral philosopher seeks to persuade us that we ought in the interests of concreteness to neglect the study of words like "good" and concentrate on words like "industrious" and "courageous". The object of such a manoeuvre might be to convince us that *all* moral words have their descriptive meaning irremovably attached to them; but, fortunately for the usefulness of moral language in expressing changing standards, this is not so.' Hare says later on, 'The account would suffice for the language of an irrevocably closed society, in which a change in moral standards was unthinkable; but it does not do justice to the moral language of a society like our own, in which some people sometimes think about ultimate moral questions and in which, therefore, morality changes. Orwell's Newspeak in *1984* was a language so designed that in it dangerous thoughts could not be expressed. Much of Oldspeak is like this, too – if we want, in the Southern States (sc. of the USA) to speak of a negro as an equal, we cannot do this by addressing him as a nigger; the word "nigger" incapsulates the standards of the society, and, if we were confined to it, we could not break free of those standards' (*Freedom and Reason*, p. 25). The comparison between people who are firmly wedded to the use of 'courageous' as a term of praise and people who are firmly wedded to

[1] See 'Morality as a system of hypothetical imperatives', *Philosophical Review* (1972); 'Moral Beliefs', *Proceedings of the Aristotelian Society*, vol. 59 (1958–59); 'Goodness and Choice', *PAS Supplementary Volume* (1961).

the use of 'nigger' as a term of contempt is not casually made: Hare reverts to it *prudens et sciens* in a passage too long to quote (pp. 187–91).

Such thoughts are in the air of our pluralistic society; and Hare is only a typical specimen of those philosophers who, in a very different sense from the Gospel use of the phrase, have not come into the world to condemn the world. We may notice the suggestion that because 'some people sometimes think about moral matters', morality may be expected to change on such matters as whether courage is to be reckoned a virtue: as though having firm, settled, convictions on such matters meant *not* thinking about them; as though Aristotle and Aquinas were paradigm cases of non-thinkers. This sort of stuff is all too familiar. Of course whether it is good for people to keep changing their thoughts about moral matters

> As though our standards were intended
> For nothing else but to be mended –

depends on the goodness or badness of the thoughts they started with; and if approval should not be firmly associated with the epithet 'courageous', it certainly ought not to be firmly associated with calling a man a 'moral pioneer' or 'moral reformer'.

It appears indeed that Hare wishes to depreciate the value of courage, at any rate of 'so-called "physical" courage'. He thinks it would be 'a hazardous claim' that this moral quality is 'upon the whole conducive to human well-being'; on the contrary, 'in the present state of military science', the possession of courage may not be really needful or desirable (p. 149). This emphasis on

military examples of courage (cf. also p. 187) may come from an Oxonian preoccupation with the *Nicomachean Ethics*. But even if we confine ourselves to military examples, Hare's thesis is sufficiently absurd. It is as if he seriously defended the standards of Gilbert's Topsy-turveydom in *The Bab Ballads*:

> Where vice is virtue – virtue, vice

so that for example

> A soldier – save by rarest luck –
> Is always shot for showing pluck:
> That is, if others can be found
> With pluck enough to fire a round.

But I see no reason to believe that as yet physical courage has no utility for a soldier; and a modicum of physical courage is needed in civilian life – let us say, to ride a bicycle in city streets.

I can see no logic compelling a man who thinks 'courage' is clearly a word one rightly uses in praise to think likewise that 'nigger' is a word rightly used to express contempt. Is Hare then simply putting the man who commends courage and the man who despises negroes side by side in the dock, with a view to getting a 'guilty' verdict against both? Apparently not. He puts into the mouth of 'recent naturalists' an argument that the evaluation which normally goes with the word 'courageous' is tied to the meaning of the word. Against any 'naturalist' who did use such an argument, Hare might be able to reason *ad hominem* that at that rate one 'logically' cannot but despise a negro, given the evaluation that goes with the word 'nigger' (p. 188). But when I say that courage is clearly and certainly a virtue, I do

not say this is true by reason of the very meaning of the word 'courage': so Hare can find no fulcrum by which to lever me from a position I hold to a position I abhor.

Indeed, I should not say of any proposition – except one explicitly about the meaning of words – that it was 'true in virtue of what the words employed mean': I find such talk philosophically pretty well useless. And I shall digress for a moment from my main topic to say why I find such talk useless: clearing rubbish out of the way makes for the good health of philosophical discourse in general, and is certainly not a superfluous task in moral philosophy.

Obviously the most crassly empirical remark may owe its truth to the meaning of words. Imagine a chivalrous English gentleman testifying in a New York court on behalf of his friend who is accused of manslaughter with a car. 'O yes,' he says in reply to counsel's question, 'the pedestrian was definitely standing on the pavement and not looking when the car hit him': so his friend is acquitted on this testimony from an honourable man. Here it makes all the difference to the truth of what is said whether 'pavement' bears its English or its American sense: English 'pavement' = US 'sidewalk', US 'pavement' = English 'roadway'. But of course *this* way for a thing one says to be true (or false) 'in virtue of what words mean' is not what people *want* to mean when they use the phrase in philosophy. They want to have pure samples in which the meaning of the words used is the *only* source of truth in what is said. This is what I regard as an unclear and unusable notion.

In discussion of this matter, hackneyed examples tend

to recur: one such is 'Any father is male'. But an equally likely example is what Quine has called the sempaternity thesis: 'Once a father, always a father' or more long-wordedly 'If A is ever father of B, then A is always so so long as A and B both live'. Either of these might easily be given as a specimen of something true in virtue of the meaning of words. But if both are true, let alone true by virtue of the meaning of words, then also it is true that if A is father of B, A cannot cease to be male and become female so long as B lives; as a general proposition of biology this is certainly false, its truth is disputed even as regards human beings, and anyhow it is not true in virtue of the meaning of the words used.

These are not examples that I have gratuitously wished upon upholders of a strict analytic/synthetic distinction. They often spontaneously use one or other premise of my paradoxical argument as a good clear example of truth in virtue of meaning; I have several times then caused astonishment and outrage by producing my argument when I happened to be present. There are of course various escape routes. One might reject one of the premises as false: to leave it as true but only synthetically true would be unavailing, for on the face of it if both premises are *true*, whether by virtue of meaning or not, then the conclusion follows, and the conclusion is false. But if this is the line taken, then what intuitively is true in virtue of the meaning of words may not even be true. Or again one might say that both premises are true and true in virtue of the meaning of words but the term 'father' does not mean the same in both. But this again shows that our intuitions about truth in virtue of mean-

ing are extremely unreliable even in simple cases; for one may bet that but for my paradox the suggestion that 'father' needs disambiguating would not have been made – or not by your average philosopher. (A biologist of course could never be caught in this sort of trap, being professionally aware how inadequate familiar terms like 'father', 'male', etc. are to capture the complexities of the living world.) If in such a simple case a change in the meaning of a concrete term can escape notice, very little reliance can be put on claims to produce something 'true in virtue of meaning'. And I need not have restricted myself just to these examples; you may find plenty more in the literature, e.g. in Waismann's well-known series of articles 'Analytic–Synthetic'.[1]

I have digressed from the topic of the virtues, but not from what is important in moral philosophy. Many moral philosophers have invested a lot of their intellectual capital in the unsound, watered stock of dubious semiotic theories; this is true in particular of those who appeal to supposed differences between kinds of meaning that terms can have. I have compared the logician's role in philosophy to an accountant's; the realistic valuation of investments in the analytic/synthetic distinction would make it obvious that more than one well-known moral philosopher is intellectually bankrupt.

Back then to my main question. I am not prepared to regard the characterization of prudence, justice, temperance and courage as virtues in the aspect of a revisable thesis; but let no more be said of my therefore making it

[1] Now reprinted in Waismann, *How I see Philosophy* (Macmillan, 1968)

'true by definition' or 'true by virtue of the meaning of words', or of my being committed by parity of reasoning to accept racialist terms of contempt into my vocabulary.

Why do men need the virtues? I have on record two shots in this general direction in the past: one in my paper 'Good and Evil', one in 'The Moral Law and the Law of God', reprinted in *God and the Soul*. I argued that there is no good sense to be made of an appeal from Inclination to the Sense of Duty. A man may indeed *feel* that he *must* do something, his not to reason why, or contrariwise that he *must* avoid something: but such feelings may notoriously be induced by childish traumas or be directed towards or away from almost any sort of action by education; in so far as a man is restrained by such inhibitions he is not a rational agent. It may belong to the *salus rei publicae* that there should be many men thus irrationally restrained, so long as what they avoid doing really is bad: as Spinoza said, *terret vulgus nisi terretur*, and many men no doubt would immediately behave much worse if their irrational inhibitions were removed. I shall not discuss the casuistry of trying to make men more rational; but Christ's words about pearls before swine suggest that over preaching the Gospel, still more over just preaching rationality, one should observe a certain caution in the choice of audience.

What Kant said about intrepidity, I say about conscientiousness: the conscientiousness of a villain like Himmler, his triumph over his own feelings in order to do monstrous deeds, only makes him more detestable. I have no reason to think Kant would have disagreed: for someone who has Kant's Good Will is not only con-

scientious but *right*. Or again: few readers of *Huckle-berry Finn* would not rejoice in imaginatively contemplating the way Huck's decent Inclination to help the fugitive negro boy Jim keeps on overcoming the Sense of Duty that naggingly tells him to cease and desist. A rational consideration propounded to an agent must, I said, relate to his Inclinations. Does this mean that in answering the question why men need the virtues I have to show that each man is profited by being virtuous in these respects, or at least has the best rationally estimable chance of profit? It does not. A man normally does not want things only for himself; nor did I ever imply that, to be shown rational, a policy must be justified in terms of what a man wants for himself.

So far I have nothing to recant: but in my previous papers I failed to draw an important distinction regarding Inclinations. The distinction I must admit to having blurred is the distinction between two senses of want or inclination: namely, the 'desire' sense and the 'need' sense. For this I am now trying to make amends: that is why I put 'need' into my title. If we reject the Sense-of-Duty sense of 'must' as a possible explanation of the word, need is a teleological notion: necessity for the attainment of an end.

We are familiar with the type of reasoning which starts from some aim or policy laid down as a premise and proceeds step by step to infer the means of securing the aim, carrying out the policy. The logical structure of such reasoning, and its relation to the structure of deductive propositional reasoning, is not yet fully a matter of agreement, but we may reasonably hope that

the matter will be cleared up. Aristotle's doctrine of teleology is that if we speak as if Nature had aims or policies we may work out what happens in the world by constructing reasonings formally parallel to human practical deliberations. Because most of his examples, even in biology, can be faulted for inadequate natural knowledge, the Aristotelian doctrine has been much blown upon. All the same, I think, it can be strongly defended, and the common attacks upon it are quite worthless.

It should be clear from the way I have stated it that an Aristotelian teleological explanation does not ascribe either something like desire to inanimate natural agents, or a contrivance of means for ends to Almighty God. Hobbes's witticisms about how a pane of glass, if it knew what it would be at, would stay in the window and not fall into the street, may have hit at the doctrine of his contemporaries, but leave Aristotle untouched.

We may equally scout the idea that teleological explanation of this sort involves Divine adaptation of means to God's ends. By his free and unaccountable will, God produces a universe within which some teleological explanatory schemes actually work. But God has no need either of achieving the end formulated in the first premise of such a schema, since he is perfect and changeless, or of using means to the end; the reproduction of living things is manifestly teleological in its pattern, but God can get as many insects or elephants or oaks as he wants by merely dreaming them up, without any reproductive mechanism, since he is an Almighty Creator. The role of teleological explanation is not to add to the corpus of natural theology.

Nor are teleological explanations barren or scientifically useless. They often have heuristic value in biology: quite recently, J. Z. Young explained the present role of the human pineal gland by making the heuristic assumption that it wouldn't be there ('evolution' wouldn't have 'let' it survive!) if it had no function.

Lastly, teleology is not straightforwardly incompatible with mechanism. An old-fashioned mechanical clock is a paradigm both of Newtonian explicability by efficient causes and of explicability in terms of what it is for – to tell the time – and of the way its parts subserve this end. This would of course still be true of a clock we unexpectedly found on arrival in the sandy desert of Mars; we need no information or conjecture about the existence and nature of Martians in order to satisfy ourselves that the clock is a complex mechanism *de facto* describable by elaborating a teleological analysis of its structure and movements.

Even in inanimate natural objects not formed into machines, teleology cannot be excluded from scientific accounts of their behaviour: I quote Poincaré's *La science et l'hypothèse* (p. 154; my translation):

> The mere formulation of the Principle of Least Action has something about it that shocks our mind. In order to move from one point to another, a material molecule removed from the action of any forces but constrained to move on a surface will take the geodetic, i.e. the shortest, course.
>
> The molecule seems to know which point it is meant to be brought to, to foresee the turn it will take to reach that point, following such-and-such a course, and then to choose the most convenient course. This formulation

therefore presents the molecule to us as an animate, free, being, and clearly needs to be replaced by a less shocking formulation, one in which (as philosophers would say) final causes would not seem to take the place of efficient causes.

Poincaré's shock and worry is quite inappropriate. It is indeed quite natural to present reasoning according to the Least Action principle in this teleological form, with premises 'The particle is to pass from point A at time t_1 to point B at t_2' and 'Of paths from A to B, that one is to be followed for which the action is least over the path'; but as we have seen, such a style of presentation does not imply either crude animism or crude deism with a sort of engineer God. This is not the only case where teleological presentation is natural and helpful. Reasonings according to Le Chatelier's principle, about the behaviour of an equilibrium system subjected to a new constraint and then acting as it were *in order* to restore equilibrium, are also naturally cast in the teleological form. If I knew more physics I am sure I could multiply examples.

I maintain then that this teleological way of thinking, conducted on essentially Aristotelian principles but without his obsolete natural science, is intellectually respectable. And in that way of thinking it makes good sense to ask 'What are men for?' We may not be so ready with an answer, even a partial answer, as when we ask 'What are hearts for?' 'What are teeth for?'; but Aristotle is right to my mind in desiderating an answer – the success in bringing men's partial organs and activities under a teleological account should encourage us to think

that some answer may be found. But not as quickly as Aristotle thought: it does not show straight off what men are for if we know that men and men only are capable of theoretical discourse.

But in order to show that men need virtues to effect whatever men are for, it may turn out unnecessary to determine the end and the good of man. For people whose first practical premises, formulating their ultimate ends, are not only divergent but irreconcilable may nevertheless agree on bringing about some situation which is an indispensable condition of either end's being realized, or on avoiding some situation which would prevent the realization of either end. That is what compromise means, that is what diplomacy is in aid of.

Consider the fact that people of different religions or of no religion at all can agree to build and run a hospital, and agree broadly on what shall be done in the hospital. There will of course be marginal policy disagreements, e.g. about abortion operations and the limits of experimentation on human beings. But there can be agreement on fighting disease, because disease impedes men's efforts towards most goals.

Of course such compromise agreement can be achieved only so long as there is not too violent disagreement about ultimate ends. A Christian Scientist would not agree about the hospital. But then, if a Christian Scientist takes his religion seriously, he must disagree about a great deal that the rest of us believe about how things are in the world. Why should I take the one deviant opinion more seriously than the other? At this point I shall be told that facts and values are very different.

There are decision procedures like weighing and measuring for getting agreement about facts; there are no decision procedures by which to enforce agreement about values. This is an old story in philosophy; it goes right back to Plato's *Euthyphro*. It is none the better for being old.

We can in fact sometimes and in important matters come to an agreement about policies and values; only this makes possible the measure of peace and civilisation that exists in the world. Here, as about factual matters, we disagree only against a background of agreement; it is an error of method in moral philosophy to concentrate on what is problematic and disputable rather than study the methods of reaching agreement; imperfect and unsystematized, but not negligible.

On the other hand, there may be irresoluble disagreement about matters of fact: observation, memory, and testimony are all fallible. For an instance of this, we need only consider a legal wrangle about a traffic accident: people will dispute about just what happened, and also about what would have happened if suitable avoiding action had been taken; and there is no decision procedure for reconciling such disputes.

The thesis of the intractable nature of disputes about values, and of radical difference between these and disputes about facts, is often supported by a curiously circular argument; I believe Alan Gewirth was the first to notice this. When we say everybody agrees on some proposition of physics, we know very well, if we will clear our mind of cant, that 'everybody' is a mere figure of speech; huge numbers of people on Earth will have

heard of the matter, but among those who have only a minority are really competent to form an opinion, the rest accept it on authority. This holds good even for such notorious facts as that the Earth is round and the Sun a huge ball millions of miles away. But when it is a matter of practical judgment, then, some philosophers would have us think, anybody's and everybody's opinion must be fairly polled; we must consult the Christian Scientists, the Azande, the Trobriand Islanders, Herr Hitler, old Uncle Joe Stalin and all. It is not at all surprising that there is a very different result of the poll when a very different lot of people are being polled.

To this the reply will be made that the resort to a different population for the opinion poll is justified because in morality, unlike questions of fact or of mathematics, there are no experts or authorities; one man has as much right to an opinion as another. But how do we know this? Because moral questions are radically different from factual questions? If this is the answer, the supposed differences between moral and theoretical disagreements are going to be what justify the different ways of taking an opinion poll; then we are running in a vicious circle if we use the results of the different opinion polls to support the thesis that moral disagreement is less resoluble than theoretical disagreement.

As for the view that there is no such thing as moral expertise: we very commonly judge that A is a fool, who follows no counsel but his own, or equivalently follows the counsel of flattering friends who will advise him to do what anyhow he wants to do; that B is wise enough to seek the genuine counsel of others; that C is wise in

practical affairs and his counsel is rightly sought eagerly by other men. We make the same sort of distinctions about different degrees of knowledge in theoretical matters. In both cases what makes a man's reputation and value for consultation is partly natural flair, partly experience.

I peremptorily exclude from discussion sufficiently crazy moral views, on the same footing as sufficiently crazy theoretical views. There is a sufficiency of theoretical and practical consensus between men, these exclusions once made, for people of diverse opinions to cooperate in building houses and roads and railways and hospitals, running universities, and so on. And on the basis of this consensus we can see the need of the four cardinal virtues to men: these virtues are needed for any large-scale worthy enterprise, just as health and sanity are needed. We need prudence or practical wisdom for any large-scale planning. We need justice to secure cooperation and mutual trust among men, without which our lives would be nasty, brutish, and short. We need temperance in order not to be deflected from our long-term and large-scale goals by seeking short-term satisfactions. And we need courage in order to persevere in face of setbacks, weariness, difficulties, and dangers.

D. Z. Phillips and others of that school will protest at my not taking a high Stoic line about virtues being prized for their own sake and not for the benefit they bring to man. There are frequent attacks from this side upon Philippa Foot for trying, and of course failing, to show at this level of discourse that virtues always 'pay' their bearers. Mrs Foot is well able to look after herself;

but I too have been the target of this sort of attack, and I shall briefly reply. It is mere sophistry to confuse the thesis that men need the cardinal virtues for their benefit – that we can see this without determining specifically what men are for – with the thesis that being brave or just must pay the individual brave or just man. Men need virtues as bees need stings. An individual bee may perish by stinging, all the same bees need stings; an individual man may perish by being brave or just, all the same men need courage and justice. It is equally sophistical to write as if the alternatives were: moral virtue for its own sake, and selfishness. Men are so made that they do care what happens to others; quite apart from respect for Duty, that is the way men's Inclinations go. And Hume pointed out, in a passage quoted by Mrs Foot, that it is precisely our concern for others that may tempt us not to observe justice: say, to divert to B money justly due to A, because A is a miser or profligate whom the money could not benefit, whereas B could benefit greatly.

The need of men for faith, hope, and charity could be established only by a far more specific determination of man's end. Of charity I will not now speak much. If charity is love of God above all things in the world and of our neighbours for God's sake, charity is to be prized only if there is a God: otherwise it is a pathetic delusion like Don Quixote's love of Dulcinea. The word 'charity' bears other senses, but it is dubious whether in these senses charity is a virtue at all.

On the other hand, we can perhaps see that faith and hope *may* be needed without determining man's place in

the world and last end. For it may be that not all men attain the end that men are for. The teleological explanation of an acorn is that it is growing into an oak; but most acorns do not become oaks. It has been held that whether men attain their chief end or not nowise depends on human choice; perhaps all men do anyhow, perhaps some men are predestined to fail. But if (and this is what I believe) all men can attain their last end, but only by right choices, then it is reasonable to suppose that the right choice must be guided by a right view of things. And to hold on to the right view of things even when (as McTaggart puts it) it seems too good or too bad to be true: that requires a virtue in the will, to resist temptations to wishful or fearful thinking. So in a general way, independently of any very definite view of what men are for, we can see that a virtue may be needed fulfilling the role that medieval theology gave to faith; McTaggart, whose view of man was very different from a medieval Christian's, in fact used the name 'faith' for the virtue that enables us to hang on to a right view of things when we have once attained it and not be deflected from that vision by the changes and chances of our mortal life. It is easier still to explain what role the virtue of hope may have: if attainment of man's chief end is possible but arduously difficult, we need a virtue that preserves us alike from a fatuous presumption that blinds us to the difficulties and dangers of the path, and from despair that would make us give up, lie down, and miserably perish.

I have tried to expound men's need of the virtues in terms of what men are for, their inbuilt teleology. One

reply to this might be 'What of it? You have only described what by metaphor may be called Nature's intentions for man. But why should we care about these if they conflict with our intentions and our freely adopted values? Nature, as the Victorian radical Place put it, is a dirty old toad.'

Of course a man is free to 'know good and evil' in what I am told is the sense of Genesis; to lay down his own standards, regardless of his inbuilt teleologies. The trouble is that it will not work out. Nature is such that one living thing lives by destroying and consuming other life, and of course this is one of the things that make all men call Nature a dirty old toad or the like. But if some-one decided to be a conscientious objector to this arrangement, he would soon have to choose whether to endure the pangs of conscience or of hunger. If this objection went so far as stopping the phagocytes in his blood from destroying alien life, he would die quickly and nastily. Other moral standards at odds with what by nature men are for would lead to disaster less quickly and less dramatically but no less surely. This, in Biblical language, is the wrath of God coming upon the children of disobedience: which is not a matter of an irascible Nobodaddy above the clouds, but of the daily experience that fools who persist in their folly are not spared the natural consequences, though by God's mercy the disaster may be delayed.

2

FAITH

'Without face you cannot be shaved.' Legend tells that the holy priest who received John Henry Newman into the Roman communion used to say this as he went around England preaching to derisive and hostile audiences. I have taken it as my motto for this chapter because I want to emphasize that the need for the virtue of faith if we would be saved is a matter of internal relation, like the impossibility of shaving off a beard if there isn't a face to shave it off; it is not that God grudges his grace and mercy to all who cannot achieve at least an O-level pass in a compulsory theological examination.

The four cardinal virtues can be seen to be necessary for the achievement of man's chief end, of what men are for, without our needing to determine what men are for. As Kotarbiński has said in one of his neat epigrams, believer and unbeliever can be loyal colleagues in the fire brigade. Of course one ought to add that this possibility of cooperation on means between people whose ultimate ends differ, and the consequent need of the virtues that make such cooperation possible, will cease to obtain if someone holds a sufficiently deviant view of the end. The worshipper of a Monarch of Flame would not be a reliable colleague in the fire brigade. But I argued in the last chapter that one need not be speculatively deferential

to really crazy practical views any more than to really crazy theoretical views.

For the three theological virtues, on the other hand, it is impossible to establish their necessity without ceasing to hedge about what men are for. But Christians believe that man is in fact aimed at a trans-natural goal, one not determinable just in terms of the observed or inferable capacities of human nature. The chief end of man, says the Scottish Shorter Catechism, is to glorify God and to enjoy him for ever. If this is so, we appear to be caught in a vicious circle over establishing the need of faith; only someone who already has the virtue of faith will rightly grasp what the chief end of man is and why, therefore, faith is needed to attain it.

The circle, however, only exists if I attempt to demonstrate the need of faith, and I shall not do that: I shall attempt no more than to present the matter in a coherent way, and to answer, directly or by anticipation, objections against this view of faith as a virtue. I hope that for some of my readers I may thus serve to remove obstacles to faith: faith can come only by God's gift.

Without faith no salvation. To conceive what this means we need to understand both what men are saved *for* and what men are saved *from*. When we say that the knowledge and love of God is man's chief end, we are not saying that all men must attain that end, nor yet that in so far as men ever fail to attain it God is frustrated. In giving teleological explanations or descriptions, let me emphasize once more, we are not conceiving of God as a Paleyan watchmaker God who craftily contrives means to ends: such a notion of means and ends has no

application to an Almighty Creator, who neither has anything to gain from creation nor need use any means to achieve ends that he could produce by his mere will.

'The everlasting enjoyment of the vision of God is man's chief end' is a proposition like 'To grow into an oak is an acorn's chief end.' The reproductive processes of living things conspicuously lend themselves to teleological description, and conspicuously resist the easy alternative way of thinking that would explain away ostensible teleologies in terms of natural selection; for unless the mechanisms that enable organisms to reproduce after their kind – this including an inheritance of the very reproductive method itself – are presupposed, there are not going to be any organisms for any evolutionary process to work on. But most acorns, for example, do not grow into oaks. This does not mean that God's design is frustrated or foolishly wasteful: wastefulness is a nonsensical accusation against God who is inexhaustibly rich, and acorns that fail of their chief end play their part in the ecology of the forest, which again admits of teleological description. So also, men who fail of their chief end are not allowed to be useless. As Spinoza said, in the style of Hebrew prophecy: 'the ungodly are like tools in the hand of the Artisan; they serve unwittingly, and in serving they are consumed'.

But this account leaves out, thus far, one vital point: the rational creature is aimed not just at achieving a certain end, but at achieving it by its own free choice. An acorn may fail of its chief end by reason of innumerable exterior obstacles: exterior determination of a man's free choice is a contradiction in terms. Only by perverse

free choice can a man fail of his chief end: and everybody gets a genuine chance – in theological jargon,
sufficient grace – to attain his chief end by the right free
choice.

That men choose wrongly is a dark mystery, in this
life not to be fully understood. It is a mistake to explain
it by the mere existence of free choice, as apologists have
often rashly done. God, whose choice and election is
supremely free, cannot choose amiss; nor could God's
Son in his earthly life, who boldly asked his enemies
which of them could accuse him of sin; nor can the
Blessed in heaven, serving him whose service is perfect
freedom. The error here partly comes from a false moral
philosophy, which teaches that anyone who does not do
the unique act which is optimific in his circumstances is
acting wrongly; I shall have more to say about this error
when I come to discuss the virtue of prudence. For the
moment I simply affirm that an agent often has a choice
between diverse goods, so that he does no wrong whichever way he chooses, and accordingly freedom of choice
does not sufficiently explain the possibility of choosing
evil.

A Christian will believe that God allowed the possibility of evil choice, and indeed its actuality on an
enormous scale, because only so could great goods be
produced which far outweighed both the suffering and
loss caused by sin and the malice of the sin itself. For
this to be true, the relation of the good to the evil must
be an internal relation: the good must be a reaction to
the evil, so that it logically could not exist were the evil
not there. But in part we can see how this is so; how

the redemptive love in the human heart of Christ, and in the hearts of those who the Apostle says 'make up what is lacking in the suffering of Christ', outweighs all the malice of men, even the malice provoked by this very love.

I have been naturally led to the question what men are saved from. Men are saved from sin, from the evil of their own perverse will. But it is not adequate just to think of men as individually making evil free choices: the whole human race, according to Christian teaching, is involved in the enormous calamity of Original Sin. Long ago, the first ancestors of the human beings now living, the first animals raised to the dignity of rational creatures, sinned deliberately and grievously, and by their fault the entire human stock coming from them was and is corrupted. There is no salvation by solidarity with the human race: in Adam all die. It is a modern corruption of Christianity to teach that this rotten old stock has been redeemed and revivified; only those who are cut off from Adam's tree – and to this, unlike plant cuttings, they must consent freely – and grafted into the new olive tree of Christ can hope to live. The gate, as an old Christadelphian friend of mine once said, is narrow enough, it admits just one at a time. For those who want the pleasure of going with the crowd, there is only the broad road to destruction. Salvation is a matter of individual decision to respond to God's calling.

How then is Original Sin inherited? I think we may reject out of hand the story told by certain Roman Catholic apologists; that it is simply a matter of men's *not* inheriting certain remarkable privileges which by deliberate sin the first human beings forfeited for them-

selves and their descendants. The parallel employed is that of someone who may sadly reflect 'I, and my descendants after me, would all have been noblemen, if our ancestor's patent of nobility had not been annulled for high treason centuries ago.' There is on the face of it a wide difference between the mild regret that such a view of the matter would arouse, and the feeling of desperate need for a remedy that comes out in the statement of the Penny Catechism: that out natural inclinations are prone to evil from our youth up, and if not checked by prayer and penance will certainly lead us to Hell. And I need not discuss whether the story of forfeited nobility is 'a legitimate development', a 'rethinking', of the older doctrine.

I turn to one formulation of the older doctrine: Aquinas's. This formulation does not lack sternness in the presentation of man's lamentable fall and need for grace; but on the face of it Aquinas's position is inconsistent. We seem to be able to extract from him propositions forming an inconsistent pentad:

1 Original Sin is sin.
2 Sin is a matter of the soul's will.
3 The soul is directly created by God each time a new human baby comes to be in the womb.
4 The soul is not created sinful.
5 The soul cannot contract sin through becoming the soul of a body which descends from sinful ancestors. (Aquinas is committed to this because he expressly accepts the teaching of Ezekiel: that nobody incurs guilt from the sins of his father, except by choosing to follow in his father's footsteps.)

As here stated, Aquinas's theses involve a Platonic way of speaking about soul and body, which conflicts with Aquinas's own deliberately adopted Aristotelianism. One may well wish that Aquinas had been bolder in saying that Platonizing dicta of the Fathers are to be charitably expounded not imitated; that he had not so often imitated them himself. We cannot coherently think of a soul as being first created, then infused into the body, in the Aristotelian framework; not even in some sense of logical or conceptual priority. There is no such thing as the human body – it is not even *one* body – unless by the soul it already has a single life; on the other hand, the soul cannot be individuated and distinct from other souls except in virtue of being the soul of *this* body rather than another.

We may, however, properly speak of a special Divine intervention as being involved every time a new human life comes to be; this is the insight of the creationist view that we need to preserve. For the modes of description needed for human intellectual activities, language, and institutions are *logically* different from those that will serve to describe the facts and laws of sub-human nature. If so, then no logic can derive from the facts and laws of sub-human nature an explanation of human nature. Every time a human baby, capable of acquiring human intellectual capacities, comes to be out of 'the slime of the Earth', out of a blob of protoplasm, we ought to wonder at it and say: This is the finger of God. A man does not consist of two pieces, a material and an immaterial one, Divinely fitted together and later separated at death; but for all that, men are by nature children of

God, in a sense Gods as the Psalmist said, and can call God their Father more truly than any earthly father is. St Paul did not shrink from citing a pagan poet: 'We are also his offspring.' This we must not forget, even though for their sins men must 'come to destruction and perish like the princes'.

I cannot here develop the logical difference I have alluded to; Quine has anyhow done the work for me in *Word and Object* and other writings. He insists that there is no logical bridge from the propositions of natural science to the language involving indirect-speech constructions that we naturally use to describe our own and our fellows' attitudes and meanings. Determined to maintain the omnicompetence of natural science, Quine then resorts to a 'double standard', reminiscent of the 'double truth' doctrine combated by Aquinas. In our most honest and rigorous intellectual mood, inspired by the severer muse (Urania,[1] as in Tennyson?), we eschew the complex indirect-speech constructions needed for familiar discourse about the things men say and think and intend, and confine ourselves to natural-scientific descriptions of human physical reactions. The familiar locutions only *seem* intelligible; they cannot seriously be regarded as propositions with truth-values; rather, when X says what someone thinks or intends, X is dramatically enacting the part of a man in a certain attitude, and coming out with words appropriate to express the attitude he is enacting.

I have remarked in other writings on the characteristic type of theory, specially favoured in Oxford, that

[1] Urania speaks with darken'd brow – *In Memoriam*.

devalues ostensible propositions to mere performances, appraisable only (say) as felicitous or infelicitous, not as true or false. It seems not accidental that Quine's work on *Word and Object* was partly done in this philosophical milieu. The dramatic virtuosity, whereby one man in his time plays many parts, would be great indeed as regards a sentence like 'Quine denies that Geach is right in ascribing to Quine the interpretation of Frege as saying . . .'; the speaker would have to be enacting the part of Quine enacting the part of Geach enacting the part of Quine enacting the part of Frege; and it is doubtful whether such an embedded construction as I have just used could itself be allowed by the 'severer muse'. But indeed the whole theory is as incredible as McTaggart's metaphysical commitment to a denial that there is anything more than an illusory introspective appearance of discursive thought – a belief that there are no beliefs, an inference that there are no inferences.

Since it is logically impossible to explain in natural-scientific terms the origin of a new human being endowed with rationality and free will, the problem posed by Aquinas's inconsistent pentad seems to recur in an even severer form. If God is the one whose special action is required for the advance from the merely biological to the human level, and men are born with perverse and damnable inclinations, how is God not the author of their sin? Or again: Sin is of the will; but the foetus in the womb is incapable of free action; how then can it contract original sin?

I think we shall find the key to the problem if we dare to be more Aristotelian than Aquinas; in a sense, more

Aristotelian than Aristotle, for what we have to do is to reject, as Aristotle never did quite reject, the Platonic myth of parts of the soul. The *appetitus naturalis* that expresses itself in all the teleology of life, and the will that expresses itself in deliberate voluntary action, are not ascribable to different principles of life but only to one. The movement of generation, ascribable to the will of fallen Adam, continues itself in the very root of will, the *voluntas ut natura*, in any new human individual.

What was properly sin was the act of the first human beings, whereby the powers of body and mind came to be no longer harmoniously subject to a holy will; henceforth man's generative teleology was only towards offspring who should be without that harmony, whose very first motion of life was set to embody the sinful will of Adam no less than if they had been literally his members. Indeed, it is only to gross observation that the propagation of Adam's germ-plasma seems so different from (say) the propagation of a banyan tree. By nature we need to acquiesce in being the sort of flawed creatures that the Fall has made us; if we go with the tendency we fall into actual gross sin. Anybody who does not swim against the current of his human world is being swept downstream to destruction.

From this destruction, Christian belief teaches, we can be saved only by Divine grace intervening. But there is a natural precondition of salvation: we must exist as distinct individuals with our own wills. The individuation of human life is a mysterious fact, but it is certainly a fact; we are not all one person, and we are saved or lost

individually. Schopenhauer taught that though the will expressing itself in human life and generation is basically one, it becomes individualized in men through the development of the intellect, manifested physically in the brain; and precisely as thus individualized, the will becomes a possible subject of that mysterious conversion which alone can save. I think this is an essentially true insight, and I shall try to develop it.

Not every separate bit of life originating from man is an individual human being: not an ovum or spermatozoon, nor a living cell in transfused blood, nor an organ kept alive outside the body. Nor, I think, is a fertilized ovum a human being: it may develop into two or more individuals, and it may develop into what medical men call a mole, from the Latin *moles*; a lump. A mole is just that: a growing lump of living tissue. When diagnosed, a mole is removed as soon as possible; I do not think the most decided advocate of immediate animation would urge that in spite of its odd look it was a human being or perhaps several human beings. But at a certain stage of development – recognizable at the latest by the appearance of a central nervous system – the teleology of an embryo is all set to produce a new human being, a rational animal. This does not mean that the embryo then has rudimentary consciousness, as Descartes conjectured in a letter, not even that it is then capable of rational acts: rationality, as Dr Kenny has argued in his Gifford Lectures, is a capacity for *acquiring* capacities for specific rational activities. From this point on there is a new human being; his will derives in its root from the first men, but being newly individuated it *can* will

otherwise; the new intellect can enlighten the newly individuated will to do so.

Since the soul is not a separately subsisting and separately individuated entity, neither creationism nor traducianism is true as first stated. Creationism, I have argued, is right in maintaining that the advance from non-human to human life requires even now – not just once long ago – a special creative act; but we may regard this act as continued throughout the life of the species rather than repeated, even as the dependence of creature on Creator in general is continued every moment, not just confined to the beginning of the world. Traducianism is even less fitted to be taken literally, since soul cannot bud off from soul; but it is right in emphasizing the continuance in us of a life one with our first ancestors' and with its tendencies vitiated by their sin. Odd ways of generation such as are now discussed – parthenogenesis of females by females (alleged sometimes to occur naturally), cloning, or the like – could of course not alter the inherited vitiation. Only the making of a new beginning by God could produce from human stock a human being free from Original Sin: and the Gospel story of how this came about, though not strictly necessary, appears most congruous; as indeed Schopenhauer observed.

By innate disposition, as I have already said, we tend to acquiesce in being the sort of flawed creatures that the Fall has made us. Aquinas teaches that it comes the way of every man who comes to the age of reason to choose whether to remain in this alienation from God or rather to turn to God (*Summa Theologica*, IaIIae, q. 89 art. 6). Every man is given sufficient grace to make the right

choice, but many reject that grace and are lost. How this choice does come a man's way, what chances men have and how they take or reject them, we shall not know till the Day of Judgment. In the stories of the Vikings there is recorded that one Viking was named Bairnsfriend because he would not share in the popular sport of tossing infants from spearpoint to spearpoint; let us hope that he took his chance; in such ways the Grace of God may show itself despite the most corrupting environment.

The world lies in wickedness; most of what is done in the world, just because it is done on the false assumption that man's nature is basically all right and only *per accidens* faulty, is done amiss. Salvation of the individual from this corporate disaster is possible only if Divine enlightenment of the intellect makes possible a redirection of the will.

Schopenhauer held that that to which a man's will turns when he turns from his evil ways is wholly unconceptualizable, beyond the grasp of the natural human intellect, which is a mere product and manifestation of the corrupt will. This is an extreme form of the doctrine of Total Depravity. Like all forms of the doctrine, it is logically untenable: there can be pure good, but not pure evil, even in a lost angel, nor can the mind be so wholly darkened that no ray of God's truth enters. Because of this doctrine, Schopenhauer thought that the dogmas of faith were mere myths, attempts to express the inexpressible; but harmless, so long as the orientation of the will had been put right by that mysterious trans-natural change which is conversion.

Will, however, is a rational appetite: it can be

redirected only if this is made possible by a new light in the understanding; even though Schopenhauer was clearly right in saying that this cannot be enough, *velle non discitur*. And at this point there become important the considerations I brought up in my essay 'On Worshipping the Right God'. A sufficiently wrong conception of God makes it simply impossible, logically impossible, for a man's so-called love of God to latch onto God at all. However much a man's love of a woman may mean in his emotional life, he cannot be rightly said to love *her* if she is a mere *princesse lointaine* whose actual attributes he wholly misconceives and he has no real acquaintance with her.

It may be replied that whereas Dulcinea del Toboso knew and cared nothing about Don Quixote's devotion, God does know and care and may be calling and drawing a man in spite of the grossest intellectual errors. But we are told by the Apostle that we are not to believe every spirit but to try the spirits whether they are of God. If the spirit that leads a man shows itself in a sufficiently distorted conception of God, then we may have good reason to doubt that this is the Holy Spirit at all. When men believe God to be present specially in some consecrated idol, or think to serve God by ritual murder or ritual lechery, it is not the true God that they are serving: 'seeing that all the things that are done among them are false, how may it then be thought or said that they are Gods?'

The 'peoples of the Book', as Muslims say, traditionally held that a right conception of God is to be got by believing an authoritative testimony. About the nature

of belief in testimony there has been a great deal of philosophical confusion. The idea is as ludicrous as it is widespread that a man can in principle justify his rational beliefs by memory, observation and induction; his trust in the testimony of others is supposed to be inductively guaranteed. But none of us has any rational grounds *of the sort described* for trusting in the testimony of others in the way that we do and to the extent that we do. This point is concealed by a slippery use of the words 'observation' and 'experience' to mean now the observation and experience of a given individual, now human observation and experience: Hume is a conspicuous offender over this. But a moment's thought shows that a man's observation and experience cannot get him far and that the observations and experience of mankind generally are available to him only by trust in testimony and authority.

Of course not all human testimony and authority is reliable; but our standards for judgment about how reliable authorities and witnesses are are again established not by private experience and observation, but by common experience, which is itself made available only by testimony and trust in authority. This which I have just said may well create an uncomfortable feeling of our having to lift ourselves by our own bootstraps; and I shall be glad to raise a discomfort which I cannot allay, for I do not despair of people's coming to understand these matters a bit better when once they see there is a problem.

In the context of religious controversy people will say that in the end a man has to rely on his private judgment, so he may as well frankly realize he has to from the outset

and not flee to the comforts of authority; or again, that in deciding which authority to follow a man is setting himself up as a super-authority. If we consider our trust in secular authorities we ought to see that these are gross fallacies. My judgment is my judgment, true; but that is a tautology, from which nothing interesting can be inferred, and my recognizing its truth does not commit me to being my own lawyer and doctor and spurning the advice of qualified men; nor in following a lawyer's or doctor's advice am I logically committed to thinking I know more law than my lawyer and more medicine than my doctor. What justifies me, in these secular cases, in choosing some authority to follow is a most difficult epistemological question; it is not reasonable to suppose that no rationale can be found. And a man who should claim that some authority is infallible (that is, some class of authoritative pronouncements are all true) is not claiming himself to be infallible; only to be, in this instance, right.

'If we receive the testimony of men, the testimony of God is stronger.' But how, among various claimants, can we recognize the testimony of God? Certain considerations are worth mentioning. Nobody's felt conviction is a reason for demanding another's assent: Mrs Conan Doyle felt sure that there was no eternal punishment, and impressed this on her son Arthur as she sent him off to Stonyhurst, but she had no right to demand his assent. In history, testimony to a happening is worthless unless we can believe it derives by a chain of tradition from contemporaries who knew the facts. So here; we have no warrant for belief unless the chain terminates

in someone who did not believe but knew: in Moses who saw God's face, or in Christ who had all the treasures of wisdom and knowledge.

People nowadays readily speak of Christ's *faith* in his Father and his mission, even, God help us all! his faith in humanity; but if he only had faith, he walked in the dark as we do, step by step, and why should we now believe because he only believed? He was a very impressive man by any standards, but very impressive men have believed all sorts of things and cannot all have been right. Can the blind lead the blind? A long line of blind men can all perhaps keep to the road, each clinging trustfully to the one in front, if the leader of them all is sighted; if he is blind too, they will all end up in the ditch.

Again, if an authority admits to being fallible, it is fallible; one that claims to be infallible *may* be so. But a claim to infallibility carries commitments. An authority must, for one thing, insist on veracity if it would claim infallibility. No authority that excuses lying for God's sake need be considered worth a moment's attention. Only if the teaching is that a witness of the truth must *never* betray the truth, whatever the consequences, can we think that the issue of the teacher's being infallible is judicable at all. (And so a morality by which no deed whatever is excluded regardless of further consequence would mean rejection of all claims to teach infallibly. But regardless of this consideration such a morality can, I think, be shown unsound.)

Again, an authority claiming infallibility cannot also claim the right to change its mind. 'This we teach and

have always taught because it is God's truth': such a claim can perhaps be heard. 'You must interiorly assent to the assertion that p, because we make it now, although with the same authority we demanded interior belief that not-p some years ago': such a demand, if ever made, would be a staggering effrontery.

In thinking of faith as assent to dogma given by an authority, I shall encounter the protests of many good people that I ought rather to be thinking of loving trust in a Person. But the contrast is mistaken, and the ground for protest is undercut by what I have already said. The senile voter of my paper 'On Worshipping the Right God' could not be said to have a loving trust in Mr Macmillan if he had got him inextricably mixed up in his mind with the Labour hero of his youth, Mr Ramsay MacDonald; and many people's views of the Person of Christ must be as deviant from the truth as that, whatever the truth is.

It is in any case quite false to say that the faith of the Apostolic Church was a matter of believing *in* a Person *as opposed to* believing *that* something is true. The earliest creed of Christians is to be found in the New Testament: 'I believe that Jesus is the Messiah, the Son of God.' This is just as propositional as any later creed; and the evidence for its key role in the early Church is admirably set out in Hobbes's *Leviathan*, c.43.

Can we believe by faith that there is a God? This is a question for which we cannot at once jump to the negative answer if we hold that it is possible to believe, even to know, that God exists on the basis of rational arguments independent of faith. Even if we hold this

(as I do), faith may be needed to *hang on to* belief in God's existence when one is too ill or tired, or too bemused by the arguments of unbelievers, to be able to reproduce the argument. But can one *arrive at* belief in God by faith? People feel a difficulty about this from fear of running into a vicious circle; as it were, believing in the Bible because it is the word of God who is Truth, and believing that there is a God who is Truth because the Bible says so. But I think the circle can be broken and the difficulty overcome.

In the first place, there is clearly nothing irrational in calling for God's help without already believing or knowing that there is a God. A man who is lost on a mountain or in a morass does well to call for help without knowing or believing that there is a fellow-traveller able and willing to help; he will get no help unless he calls, and without help he will perish. And though the story of origins that makes the name 'Original Sin' appropriate is a matter of Christian dogma, the fact for which the name stands is written in large letters on the pages of history; who runs may read, not to read argues wilful blindness. (The Old Testament historical books are repellent to fallen man precisely because they drily, without palliation or much explicit condemnation, show what men are like; and I think Schopenhauer, and Thucydides whom 'few have loved', and Thomas Hobbes, are hated for the same reason.) Is there any hope but in the gratuitous mercy of a God? Only callous folly will laugh at the sceptic's cry 'O God, if there be a God...'

Let me shift to another parable of a man in a desperate

situation. A man in prison, facing he knows not what, receives what purports to be a message from an unknown helper. This tells him how to get in touch, and promises further help if he will only respond. Of course the letter *may* be written by a mocking jail governor or even by a suitably programmed computer; but it is not senseless for the prisoner to believe it, even though he has no independent evidence that there is this unknown friend; he is not stupidly arguing that the friend must exist and have written the letter, because that's what the letter says! And his belief may be rewarded and confirmed by further messages: even by what looks like a crack in the prison wall and a glimpse of daylight; which, Sir James Stephen remarked, means far more than the most brilliant illumination supplied by the prison authorities.

Can faith require us to accept mysteries; dogmas that we do not fully understand? Christian tradition holds this, and I shall defend the tradition; but it must not be defended for the wrong reasons. The form of *argumentum ad ignorantiam* which urges us to accept dogmas simply and solely because we are in a complete muddle about the terms involved is unfortunately one that exists elsewhere than in the unkind caricature McTaggart gives about asking people, because of their weakness of mind, to believe that the Law of Diminishing Returns devours purple quadratic equations (*Some Dogmas of Religion* §54): I know only too well what he is caricaturing. I have found the mysteries of the Trinity and the Incarnation commended to our acceptance on the ground that we have not the least idea what human personality is and still less what Divine personality is; I have found

transubstantiation similarly proposed for belief on the ground that we have not the least idea what the substance of bread is or even what the phrase 'the substance of so-and-so' means, so that if the Church solemnly assures us that one of these unintelligible entities has been replaced by another we are in no position to raise any doubt of the matter. It is puzzling enough when theologians tell us that the Persons of the Trinity are subsistent relations; but more than that, I once heard a paper defending this doctrine on the ground that relations are very peculiar entities; in fact, some of the relations things actually bear to one another are not real, though others are real; so we ought to find it credible that a relation can just *be* a person; relations are so peculiar and puzzling that we cannot rule this out in advance!

McTaggart is to my mind completely right in protesting that if we find ourselves is this sort of muddle, we ought to be sceptical until rational thought shows us a way out of the muddle, and not fancy we shall better our condition by accepting one unintelligible dogma rather than another. But there is a better way of expounding and defending the rationale of belief in mysteries that surpass our understanding; and I believe this way is also more soundly traditional.

By this account, a mystery of faith is not blankly unintelligible; even the simplest believer has some positive understanding of it, to which he can give real assent, and yet even the wisest theologian knows there is infinitely more to be learned. The mystery is not chaos and darkness visible, but a sea of light, depth beyond depth.

There will indeed be many apparent contradictions; but with regard to these we need not adopt the maxim of the legendary Scottish minister to his junior; look them firmly in the eye and pass them by! On the contrary, from the first we may be certain in principle that, as Aquinas said, arguments against the Faith are not proofs but fallacious reasonings; if we are wise enough, we shall be able to show the fallacy; to expose it as sinning against the rules not of some 'baptized reason' but of ordinary logic. *Credo ut intelligam*; without an initial venture of faith the mysteries remain permanently opaque; once that venture has been made, they more and more enlighten and strengthen the mind that contemplates them.

The question arises, however, whether the believer's conviction that his mind is being strengthened and enlightened by contemplation of the mysteries is self-deception. And here it is proper to mention a fact that the believer may well find encouraging. If what is claimed for the Christian mysteries is true, then knowledge of them ought to advance our understanding of other things, just as the Sun, too bright to gaze upon, illumines all other things we see. And just this, it may be argued, is what we do find.

In the West, even infidel philosophers are not tempted to reject the concept of a person; in fact one of them wrote a book under that very title. Theologians will sometimes tell you that this use of the word 'person' is quite different from its use in Trinitarian theology. It is not true; *our* concept of a person was forged by the theological controversies about the Trinity; and this

term, for which there is no equivalent in Plato or Aristotle, was defined in the context of those very controversies by Boethius, as 'an individual substance of rational nature'.

Again, the natural science of the Greeks was fatally held up by their way of regarding intensive magnitudes, like temperature, as due to some sort of mixture of opposites, say heat and cold. Our concept of intensive magnitude was worked out first not for the exigencies of physics but for those of theology; greater grace, or greater charity, had to be explained in terms of more of the same quality, which could vary continuously upwards and downwards without any admixture of an opposite. (Aristotle had already reached a particular case of this concept, light-intensity, and rejected the idea that brighter light means light with less darkness mixed into it; but as Richard Robinson rightly emphasizes, grasping a particular case of a concept is very different from grasping the concept itself, and Aristotle's physics is as much dominated by talk of conflicts between opposites as any other Greek's.) We may not realise how paradoxical this idea of intension and remission of forms must once have seemed; change simply in respect of a quality, not from one species of a quality to another; and this quality remains the same quality and yet changes! The Church needed this concept to defeat the Manichees; but once achieved, the concept could be used to think e.g. about intension and remission of velocity; and from medieval speculations about that we can trace a continuous chain to the thought of Galileo and on to the giant growth of modern science. How impossible electrical and thermo-

dynamic and gravitational theories would be if we were still fossicking around with ideas of warring opposites!

I could give many other illustrations: I will briefly sketch just one. I hold, and should hope to prove to neutral thinkers, that Aquinas, a theologian, was more sensitive to certain important points of formal logic than William of Ockham, who wrote treatises on logic. And the reason was that Aquinas needed a logical apparatus that would not lead him astray in the theology of the Trinity and the Incarnation. Ockham on the contrary was prepared to say that syllogisms otherwise formally valid were liable to break down if their subject-matter happened to be the Trinity or the Incarnation: a view that Aquinas would have rejected with abhorrence – one all too reminiscent of the Two Truths theory that he combated so valiantly.

I think therefore that a very good case could be made out for the thesis that the mind of Western man has been illumined and strengthened by the intellectual work of elucidating the mysteries of faith; and this suggests, though it does not prove, that God illumines the mind of the faithful like the Sun lighting up the Earth, though too bright to gaze upon with direct vision.

> Thou art the Truth; thy Word alone
> True wisdom can impart;
> It only can enlarge the mind
> And purify the heart.

The testing-point of the virtue of faith is: hanging on to the truth once received, in spite of all temptations. Even in spite of counter-evidence that seems decisive, the

man of faith must act like the hero of romance who says to his love when her innocence is triumphantly shown, 'I always believed you were innocent, even when I knew you were guilty.' And *a fortiori* he must stand firm when assailed not by rational-seeming doubts but by contingencies of life that make his creed appear too good or too bad to be true. Prosperity may make God seem superfluous, adversity may make his existence seem incredible. But the truth about God cannot change with such accidents: and whether things are near us or far away is irrelevant. If Jews could still worship their God in spite of Titus and Hadrian, they can still worship him in spite of Hitler; if Christians could believe in God after the Thirty Years' War, they can still believe in God after Hitler's war. One may pity an individual when faith is destroyed by such terrible events – there, but for the grace of God, go I! But no respect is due for authors of belly-aching books about the need for an 'agonizing reappraisal' on account of the horrors near us in space and time; such talk is solemn, but it is not serious. The world has always had much grimness in it; but the lives of the Saints, and the sure prophetical word, have always shone like candles in the dark.

3

HOPE

In my first chapter, I sketched the nature of the seven virtues I shall be discussing and the way that man needs them; I drew a distinction between the four cardinal virtues and the three theological virtues as regards the proof of their necessity. A specific answer to the question what men are for and what end they should aim themselves at is not required in order to show the need of the cardinal virtues; for very little reflection shows that in a world like ours with its perplexities, temptations, and dangers, the cardinal virtues are needed to attain any great and worthy end. It is indeed necessary to assume further that rational creatures are so constituted that whether they attain the ends they are naturally constituted for depends in part at least on whether they choose to set themselves to attain them; but this assumption again is reasonable on very various views of man's end.

That men need hope as a virtue is a doctrine depending on a much more specific conception of man's last end. Speaking of hope as an emotion, the scholastics tell us that its object is *bonum arduum*; a good possible of attainment, but only with difficulty and precariously. Now many people have held that all men sooner or later attain the end for which men are made, and others have believed that a man can in his life come to be completely certain that he himself will attain it. In either case there

could be a certainty that excluded hope. Or again, it might be held that men can fail to achieve their last end by force of circumstances, through no fault of their own: and if it were so, this would make a radical difference to our hope. The teaching of faith is that every man has a genuine chance of salvation – sufficient grace, in theological jargon – and nobody is forced to miss his last end through inculpably running into temptations beyond his strength or dilemmas from which there is no way of extricating himself; on the other hand, nobody in this life can be perfectly assured of salvation so that he need no longer fear to fall, and nobody can safely neglect a means of grace offered him, because this chance once lost may turn out to have been the last chance.

Moreover, though nobody will be tempted beyond his strength unless he culpably runs into temptation, equally nobody can be assured that he will be spared severe tribulation. The value that has come to be put on the words 'heroic virtue' is one of the things that C. S. Lewis's Screwtape could count as a triumph for the Philological Arm: people have come to think that heroic virtue is certainly not going to be required of ordinary people like them. The hard and manifest truth is that one may have to choose between doing something extremely repugnant, difficult, or dangerous and doing something extremely wicked; I shall revert to this matter in later chapters. If by choice of wickedness in such an emergency one may lose all for ever, then there can be no confidence that one will prevail; only that one can. If, as the wartime slogan says, it all depends on me and I depend on God, then I may confidently believe that my

efforts *can* achieve salvation, but a sense of my infirmity prevents my being confident that they *will*. The virtue of hope preserves a mean between despair and presumption.

I would add something about the matter of the last missed opportunity, the last neglected grace, on the part of those who are lost. On the one hand, the chance may come chronologically late and yet not be missed: and the merciful Master will pay a full reward for one hour's work in the vineyard. But perhaps there is another side to this; perhaps a man may lose his last chance when he is young, and then live to be old: live contented and at home with the world, but in God's eyes be dead. If a man is eventually lost, some chance will have been the last, and to the eternal God the length of time is nothing; whether a man seizes a chance between the saddle and the ground, or rejects it for ever in youth to become a hard, contented, worldling. This thought should induce fear, but not despair; the man who may thus have lost his last chance is not the sort of man who will go mad like Cowper with thinking that he has done so.

I have little to add about the virtue of hope; but there is much to say about hope, the hope, the one hope, in the sense of what is hoped for. Faith, I said last time, is a matter of individual decision: 'I believe', not as fashionable rewriters of the Creed would have it 'we believe'; and faith on someone else's behalf is a difficult notion. But what faith teaches the believer to look forward to is not just his own salvation but a general salvation: the just kingdom that shall have no end, the resurrection of the dead ('dead' is plural in languages that show its

inflexion), and the life of the age to come. Those who whole-heartedly enjoy solidarity with the lost race of man in this life may expect all to perish, they are on the broad road leading to destruction; he who by the individual obedience of faith turns away from the evil will that incarnates itself anew in his very birth does not go alone to the Alone, but may hope to partake in the communion of Saints.

What I shall do in the rest of this chapter is to improve this theme, as old-fashioned preachers say. It would not suit with the character of this chapter to multiply evidence from Scripture and Tradition that this is indeed the content of the hope both in the Old and New Testament dispensations, from the promises to the Patriarchs onwards. Since the character and the necessity of hope are not to be established by mere reason, as could be done for the cardinal virtues, demonstration is not to be sought: only clarification and answers to objections. What I shall try to show is that any other hope for individuals or for humanity at large, is quite unfounded: if there is not this hope, all hope is in vain.

I begin then with the hope for individuals. The first truth to be grasped here is the unfoundedness of the naturalist world-view, by which man is just a superior animal with powers evolved to meet his needs in his environment. In the last chapter I briefly sketched an argument against naturalism: the mere descriptions we regularly use for the linguistic and voluntary behaviour of men are logically not derivable from the apparatus of scientific theory that suffices for the description of irrational creatures, and therefore no naturalistic account

of linguistic and voluntary behaviour can be logically respectable. Some people have seen this, and desperately look forward to a time when natural science will have progressed so far that we shall not need, in serious thinking, to talk of people's words, opinions, plans, and intentions, but only of physical and physiological states and events! The obnoxious ways of speaking would just drop out of use, like talk about witchcraft and diabolical possession. Obviously this is only an impious hope, and there is not a shadow of reason for expecting it to be realised; and for the moment a proponent of this view can neither state his own position nor attack his adversary's without using notions that he ought to try to eliminate.

In my last chapter I referred to Quine's double-talk, inspired now by the gentler now by the severer muse. In order to bring out sharply the difficulties naturalism must present for a man with a logical conscience, just consider Quine's doctrine of the way existential commitment is expressed by the use of quantifiers and equivalent devices. I have nothing to say against this as a piece of logical theory: I disagree with Quine only marginally, and am on his side against opponents who would make chaos come again and forfeit the gains of the Frege–Russell tradition that Quine is defending. What carries existential commitment is not a language but a theory: a simple distinction, often blurred. (A language normally contains the contradictories of all its sentences; but a theory, one hopes, does not contain the contradictories of all its theses.) But the commitment of a theory in turn is really the commitment of a theorist:

existential commitment is a matter of what Mr A *says* exists, or of what Mr A would have to say exists if only Mr A were consistent. Even if I were wrong about this last point, existential commitment would still be a matter of what is *said* to exist by a theory considered as a set of sentences.

At this point, however, Quine's logical theory is at odds with his naturalism. For Quine's naturalism commits him to holding that no rigorous sense can be made of the verb 'to say' (which is incorrigibly intentional); not even if we were to take the impersonal sense of 'to say' as fundamental, the sense in which not men but sentences say things. The sad result is that Quine's weapon against ontological obfuscation loses its sharp edge; he *cannot* in disputation make clear what he means by ontological commitment, because so to do would mean bringing prominently forward a notion that the severer muse would ban; and from this lack of clarity only the foes of clarity benefit.

These considerations from the philosophy of logic may very well weigh more with me than with hearers whose thoughts are less 'abstract' in subject-matter; though I should say this illustrates the extreme concreteness and importance that McTaggart and Wittgenstein alike ascribed to such considerations. But I turn to a simpler matter: Russell's chicken, which runs every day to be fed and one day has its neck wrung. The example points up the difference between the truth and the survival-value of expectations. The chicken's inductive habit betrays it in the end, but by then it has propagated its kind, whose expectations will be equally imperfect from an intellectual

point of view and equally useful. Let us suppose (*datur, non conceditur,* as a scholastic disputant might say) that the intellectual powers and inductive habits of men are the product of natural selection: that would at best guarantee that they have the kind and degree of reliability that the expectations of Russell's chicken have. Any large-scale extrapolation to regions of space and time far distant from us, to the microscopic and the ultra-microscopic, will involve inductions that could very well be wildly unreliable without having been detrimental to the survival of the human race. The naturalist account of why our inductive procedures should be trusted is thus quite insufficient: indeed, it commits suicide, because only if large-scale extrapolation can be trusted could there be the faintest reason for believing the story of rational creatures evolving by natural selection.

Nowadays people often get excited over the prospect of making life in a laboratory out of non-living materials; there is a common impression that if this could be brought off it would be a deadly blow to the belief in a Creator and *a fortiori* to revealed religion. The impression can have arisen only from gross ignorance of the history of science: in the Middle Ages every theologian who counted believed that solar radiation generated life out of inanimate materials; and that view was finally refuted, as regards the generation of life in the present state of the Earth, by the work of men like Pasteur and Tyndall in the last century. For medieval thought the gulf that could be bridged only by Divine intervention came not between life and the inanimate, nor between consciousness and lack of consciousness, but between

rational and irrational creatures. I think there is no reason now to think otherwise – only fashion.

It is in connexion with this that we are told of the great probability that there are many other planets inhabited by rational creatures. Life must originate, we are told, wherever the physical conditions for life are favourable: and there must be so many planets on which life has originated that on millions of them rational beings will have evolved by natural selection. But rational beings cannot so come to be: the coming to be of a rational creature is strictly miraculous – it exceeds all the powers of sub-rational nature. Humeans will protest that we cannot tell what all the powers of sub-rational nature are except from experience; and experience does not support the view that sub-rational nature can produce no rational being – we see the contrary every day, when a healthy human being is born from the union of sub-rational living units. But an everyday miracle is none the less a miracle: the number of Masses said each day does not diminish the wonder that Transubstantiation would have to be.

I have argued that the sense in which the coming to be of a rational creature, with responsible discourse and free choice, exceeds all that irrational nature can do is a sense than can be made logically precise. When we hear of some new attempt to explain reasoning or language or choice naturalistically, we ought to react as if we were told someone had squared the circle or proved $\sqrt{2}$ to be rational: only the mildest curiosity is in order – how well has the fallacy been concealed? Least of all should we be impressed by the alleged human production of

artificial intelligence in machines: there is little more ridiculous than the spectacle of a man inferring, from the existence of a machine that produces language and calculations because of people's designing it and giving it a program, that human beings are themselves such machines fundamentally, only their coming to be can be explained without bringing in any notions of plan and intention.

So it is reasonable to believe that the rational creatures living here first came to be, and do daily come to be, by a special Divine intervention. Whether rational creatures are many or few, they are objects of special Divine concern: all the more because what happens in the world, God so permitting, depends not only on God's will but on the wills of what Sir Leslie Stephen called the millions of little first causes. If there are rational animals elsewhere, they are fortunately far distant from us, and their Maker's dealings with them are his business not ours: 'what is that to thee? Follow thou me'. (I say 'fortunately' for many reasons: for the moment it will be enough to mention that people who pretend to regard dolphins as rational creatures with a language nevertheless think they may experiment on them as on brutes.) In any event, the other rational creatures will not have originated from the irrational by mere natural process, any more than men did.

The dignity of rational creatures so delineated must determine what we can say about the proper object of hope in respect of their last end. It is reasonable to think of dialogue between God and his rational creatures: that they should approach God with petitions, as a man

approaches a friend, with some prospect that because of their petitions the contingencies of Nature will be otherwise ordered than if they had not asked; that God should in return guide their course in the world by making known to them his commandments and his promises. I have written elsewhere of petitionary prayer. What must now be said is that God's commandments and promises alike need not be made known to men by special revelation: they are declared also to man's natural reason.

Expectations regarding the future would fall into chaos but for trust in the promises of God, who is unchangeable in his purposes, almighty in the execution of his will, and faithful to his own word once given. When men's minds are freed from prejudice and superstition, they can formulate certain standards of rational expectation, both as regards regularities and as regards what is vulgarly called chance. But there is no logical warrant for holding that it is either certain or probable that in the course of our threescore years and ten Nature will conform to our standards; nor is it psychologically necessary for us to adhere to these standards – other cultures do not; nor can it be argued that our standards must have been reliable for us to survive – that guarantee is quite insufficient. If there is a God whose creative Wisdom is mirrored imperfectly in our own reason, and whose Providence controls both the course of events and the occasions on which we try to prognosticate it, then we can be confident that the event will not show us up as fools to have trusted our standards of rationality: otherwise we can have no such confidence. The thought may appear novel, but it is one that recurs in the Hebrew

Scriptures, where the regularities and the 'chance' events of Nature are alike ascribed to the will of God, and man's trust in the future is based on God's covenant with man that the order of Nature shall not fail.

How in this light do we regard the question whether, if a man die, he shall live again? For reason unaided by revelation the question is most baffling. God only has immortality, in the sense that the existence of any rational being other than God depends on God's will and God can bring it to an end like a tale that is told. McTaggart was surely right in seeing a positive antagonism between the aims of proving that God exists and proving that rational creatures are immortal or have an immortal part: natural immortality as often conceived involves a restriction on God's power that a theist cannot admit. On the other hand, man's mind is not tied down to the practicalities of mortal life: this is apparent even from the propensity to speculations about things widely outside the present environment and what makes for survival in it; a propensity manifested in the story-telling of the most lowly cultures. Man's mind cannot be satisfied with the here and now, and if once the idea of the Supreme and Eternal is presented to it there arises a hunger for such apprehension of it as is possible.

This must not lead us too quickly to say that the fulfilment man is for can occur only in another life than the mortal life of his body. Consider the attitude of a man like Anaxagoras or Aristotle. Even if men are mortal, they need not content themselves with the cares of this short life. Aristotle held we should side with the immortal part of ourselves; his word for this was '*athana-*

tizein'; it was formed on the model of '*mēdizein*', which meant to be a quisling who took the side of the Median invaders against his own countrymen. Just so, a man should regard his rationality as an invasion of the immortal and divine into Nature and side with the invaders as much as possible, *athanatizein*. So Anaxagoras, who saw the world as an order, *kosmos*, imposed by the omniscient and irresistible *Nous*, held that we too had a share of *nous* and it was worth having come into life in order to behold the order of things. The attitude is noble, but it leaves little room for hope: our minds can know that there is this Supreme and Eternal, in which all truth and beauty is concentrated, but this is immeasurably far short of seeing and tasting the goodness of the Lord.

It might be replied that such seeing and tasting is possible in this life, and is fulfilment enough for man: man would be fulfilled by this as a plant by flowering, and none the less because death follows, for the man as for the plant. We must not reject this view for the wrong reasons: let us recall the need to avoid the chronic confusion between the two senses of 'end'; a thing's fulfilment need not be its final stage. Union with the Divine such as would provide this sort of fulfilment is, however, very rarely claimed considering the numbers of the human race; and in most cases where the claim is made it can be rejected as fraud or delusion. Union with God by knowledge and love, *amor intellectualis Dei*, ought to show itself by enlarging the mind and purifying the heart: but who could be confident on this score that even Spinoza, let us say, attained his end? And we need not hesitate to dismiss such a claim out of hand when it is

made on behalf of men whose lives are unfruitful of virtues and whose teaching is not a mental discipline like Spinoza's, but instead darkness visible.

The upshot is that hope of attaining man's end appears very small if restricted to the course of this mortal life. Nor can I see that in the sense in which I have spoken of God's natural promises or covenants, there is a natural promise or covenant that if a man dies he shall live again. The course of nature, in which we may trust because of God's naturally known promises, gives us no reason nor hint of a reason to expect any such thing.

Men die, that is certain: they really die; it is not a shuffling off of old clothes by an underlying immortal ego. (It is remarkable how rarely men, even thoroughgoing Platonists or again professed materialists, can come to regard the dead body of a friend as a mere bit of decaying rubbish like a moth-eaten coat, fit for the municipal refuse dump.) Even if something of me survives as a separated soul, 'my soul is not I', as Aquinas said: many things I can do my soul could not do. And the very notion of the survival of a separated soul, and the unconfounded individual survival of ever so many separated souls, raise formidable difficulties, as many philosophers have pointed out.

I have written about these problems in *God and the Soul*: I shall here develop a further speculation. Traditional Christian teaching has been that the soul exists embodied after the general resurrection, but is disembodied between death and resurrection, and performs various acts of mind in this separate state. I do not wish to oppose this tradition: what I do want to question is

whether we may legitimately ask, as regards a man who has died, what his soul is doing *right now*; let us say, whether King Solomon has *yet* been released from Purgatory to Heaven (a matter on which, I hear, private revelation has been claimed). The reason for my raising this doubt is that such enquiries about the present state of a separated soul assume a one-track view of the time series; and we have good reasons to reject this view, quite apart from present concerns.

One reason is given in the chapter 'What do we think with?' of my book *God and the Soul*: it appears to me that acts of thought do not form a continuous process of change, a 'stream of thought', but are discrete and ordinally enumerable – the first, the second, the nth – and that this makes it impossible to correlate them either with separate instants or with stretches of physical time measured by the continuous local motion of bodies. I maintained the view only about thought, not about sensory processes; they, for all that I have said, may form a stream in which there is continuous change correlatable with physical processes.

I came to this doctrine of the temporal incongruence between thoughts and stretches or moments of physical time many years ago, from reading Aquinas on the relation of angelic mental acts to physical time; it is proper to acknowledge its source, though I did not cite Aquinas when I put the doctrine forward originally, for fear of arousing prejudices. Of course I am not appealing to his authority; the doctrine should commend itself to reason. It did commend itself to the reason of Norman Malcolm, in a paper I once heard him read; he argued

that a mental image could be significantly said to stand before the mind for as long as it took for a beetle to crawl across a table, but that it would be senseless to say this of a thought. I do not know whether Malcolm ever published this paper; anyhow, with no Thomist axe to grind he chose the illustration of a beetle's crawl, which exactly gives the idea of physical time as the measure of continuous local motion. A reviewer of *God and the Soul* ascribed to me belief in 'timeless events': naturally neither the phrase nor what it means is to be found in my text; I mention the misconstruction because it shows the extraordinary strength of the prejudice that the time-order must be simply unilinear and thus what is not clockable by continuous physical motion must be called timeless.

There is a second ground for positively rejecting the doctrine of unilinear time. We have to reject the supposed distinction between the future that actually is going to happen and can no more be changed or prevented than the past can, and the future that is merely going to happen but can sometimes by human effort be avoided or prevented. The adverb 'actually' is all that keeps the mere statement of this distinction from being patently self-contradictory, and in this context – since the future is on any view not yet actual – the 'actually' has no more logical force than a thump of the fist on the table. I am not saying that nothing in the future is determinate and now unpreventable, nor could I consistently say this: on the contrary, what God has promised naturally or by revelation is certainly unpreventable, for he can neither alter the past giving of his word nor break

his word, and nothing can restrain him from carrying out his will. But God's terrifying love of freedom has made the will of his creatures the hinge of fate, on which it turns whether some door of possibility shall be open or be shut for ever; perhaps the door to Heaven or Hell for somebody. There is no distinguished line of futurity, from which *all* alternativeness is excluded.

If we reject, as I think we have good reason to reject, the doctrine of unilinear time, then we cannot safely assume any longer that it makes good sense to ask what the souls of the dead are doing *now*. Perhaps it merely will be true on the day of resurrection that the man living again *did* have such-and-such thoughts, which in the time-series of his thoughts have ordinal numbers in between the last thought in his previous bodily existence and his first thought after resurrection. (This speculation has been carried further by Mary Geach in a paper published in the Spode House proceedings called 'Death and Dreaming'; she rightly, to my mind, uses as an analogy the notorious difficulties over assigning to dreams a place in the physical time-order. Of course this not to say that the experiences traditionally ascribed to separated souls are merely dreams that are to be recalled and told by the resurrected; it is only to reinforce by a further consideration the argument against unilinear time.)

If this should be true, problems about the individuation of separated souls, the place they occupy, and so on will turn out to be spurious: *whose* thoughts the thoughts in the intermediate state were will be settled by the individual identity of the man now living again. And we may similarly dismiss the conundrums about the

subject of these thoughts, the separated soul; e.g. whether it is a substance, a *suppositum*, and whether, without being a substance, it is nevertheless subsistent. The only individual substance in the case will be a man; the only genuine problem about substantial identity will be the problem how the newly risen man can be one and the same man, one and the same person, with the man who died long ago.

This is one more step in the de-Platonizing of Christian thought, a work begun by Aquinas. How alien to Christianity Platonism is, how different the Platonic and the Christian hope, comes out strongly when we contrast the Gospel stories of the Resurrected Christ with the last words Plato gives to Socrates in the *Phaedo*. Socrates dissociates the use of 'I' from any reference to his body; 'I' stands for his real self, which is only going away to live immortally. But the risen Christ reassures his Apostles 'It is I myself' – not a spirit: 'A spirit has not flesh and bones as you see me to have.' The Roman cult of the Sacred Heart calls up associations of bad art, mawkish devotion, dubious belief about the Nine First Fridays; but the central truth behind this cult is that Christ is now, as he was, truly Man; the Heart loaded with affliction, pierced with the lance, still can be moved for those he loves; and we too after death shall be true men again, for when he shall appear we shall be made like him and see him as he is.

Under Platonic influence Christians have often regarded the soul as naturally immortal and capable of beatitude independently of the body; it has thus become a matter of embarassment to explain why a soul already

perfectly blessed needs to have a body stuck on it again at the Resurrection. Confronted with this puzzle, men have fallen into two opposing errors: the mortalist heresy of the Socinians, which denies any life between bodily death and resurrection; and the heresy of Hymenaios and Philetos, which St Paul compares to a creeping gangrene, the doctrine that the resurrection has already happened, that the dead are already elsewhere in 'spiritual' bodies. Both errors are bad. The Socinian doctrine must greatly impoverish the doctrine of the Communion of Saints; the other doctrine, now very fashionable, is like the Platonic doctrine to which so many prefer it in being a mere corruption of Christianity by philosophy and vain deceit. The Socinians, or their modern successors like the Christadelphians, at least retain the traditional object of hope; the doctrine of going at death to another world in a spiritual body is an incoherent philosophical fantasy.

The doctrine of resurrection – of men living again as men – is of course itself beset with problems about identity. But these have been perversely exaggerated by some philosophers: notably by Antony Flew, who would encase himself in a panoply of philosophy against being converted though one rose from the dead. Lazarus is not, cannot be, the same person; or else he never was dead, even if he was stinking. I have found the latter alternative maintained by a modern follower of Hymenaios and Philetos; the doctrine that a man shall live again as a man was so repugnant to him that he wished to reject Lazarus as an example of a man who lived again as a man; Lazarus had not really, not 'meta-

physically', died. Going back to Flew, I can only say that his attitude deserves his own witty label, the Conventionalist Sulk. You can of course, confronted with Lazarus, *say* he is not the same man or *say* he never was dead; it does not follow that you can say it reasonably.

Lazarus is a clear and unperplexing case of life after death: the story is hard to believe but not at all hard to understand. Other cases must create difficulties. I argued in *God and the Soul* that memory could not be a sufficient criterion of personal identity; there must be both direct causal continuity of thought-processes and some sort of material continuity to preserve human individuality. The latter requirement raises old difficulties, not always merely theoretical: Aquinas's puzzle about the resurrected body of a baby born to cannibal parents and suckled by a mother living on human flesh has a grim actuality in application to the Sawney Bean family in Scotland during King James VI's reign. I do not know how material continuity is to be preserved in all cases, and I prefer not to speculate.

Difficult cases that would jeopardize the very notion of personal identity if they did arise do not therefore jeopardize it (let us never forget this) by their mere logical possibility even if they do not arise. If men rise from the dead, it will be because God raises them; and though we may dream up cases in which two persons' identities would be irretrievably scrambled, or each of two persons has an equal claim, and therefore neither a maintainable claim, to the identity of a past person, though we may fancy such things, we need not fear that our identity will thus be jeopardized. It is all in God's

hands, and God will not bungle it. If such fancies are just designed to stretch our speculative powers, well and good: if they are put forward as serious objections to the doctrine of resurrection, we may pass them by with a smile, and reply in the style of Dickens's Tommy Traddles: It isn't so, you know, so if you please we won't suppose it.

I now sum up what I have said about the hope for individual men. There can barely be a hope for an individual to attain his end, except after this life in a new life; and there is not the least ground for hoping for such a new life except for God's promise of new life in the Kingdom that is to come. This or nothing.

I end by arguing that there is no hope for men corporately either, except the promise of the Kingdom. Men in power are not to be trusted; man is a wild animal and cannot tame himself. This is the lesson of Original Sin, taught over and over again by experience in spite of all wishful thinking. It is a ludicrous delusion of our age that parliamentary democracy will somehow secure justice and freedom for all men. A Christian cannot be an anarchist; the powers that be are ordained of God, and God rules in the kingdom of men. But equally a Christian must not trust MPs or Congressmen any more than the old hereditary princes or aristocrats: must never forget God's scorn of all men governing; the truth of the text in Daniel, that God sets up over the nations the basest of men, is borne out by universal human experience.

This is not the place for a jeremiad about the many intractable problems of the world. To resolve them there

would be needed enormous wisdom and knowledge, irresistible power to see that men carried out necessary changes, incorruptible virtue that would give the lie to Lord Acton's dictum that absolute power corrupts absolutely. The idea that some committee of the miserable people now ruling the nations, aided by a team of scientific experts and perhaps by a really powerful computer, could act as a fulfilment of this Messianic ideal, is really too ludicrous for us to spend time in examining how the project would break down.

Of what Scripture calls the kingdom of men there is no hope. In contrast to this, Scripture tells us, there was and shall again be the Kingdom of God. The Jews were chosen for a unique polity, where the only king and lawgiver – and the only landowner, all men being only tenants on lease till the year of jubilee – was God himself. The Jews rejected God for their King; they would have a king after the manner of the other nations: just as now they will have a republic; and there are Jews in the Holy Land today who recognise parliamentary republican institutions as for them an apostasy, like their ancestors' demand for King Saul. But God's will is not to be thwarted by human perversity, and those who reject him only hurt themselves like a child kicking the ground.

The only hope for man, Jew or Gentile, is the universal establishment of the Kingdom of God. Concrete detailed pictures of life in that Kingdom are bound to be misleading, and I shall not try to evoke such imaginations: but our certain expectation is that the Kingdom will come, our hope can only be to have a place in it. There is no other hope. To this hope, traditional in the Jewish

people, Jews and Gentiles are turning: the poor of the world, who have long looked for a just ruler, will find that their expectation has not gone lost for ever. As the Synagogue service says:

HE AT THE LAST SHALL OUR MESSIAH SEND,
TO SAVE ALL THOSE WHO HOPE AND WAIT THE END:
HE SHALL AT LAST THE DEAD TO LIFE RESTORE:
BLEST BE HIS GLORIOUS NAME FOR EVERMORE.

4

CHARITY

I have several times attacked the view that God is lacking in perfection unless he has the attributes that count as virtues in a human being. As Aristotle remarked, it is vulgar to praise God as if he had certain human virtues: of the virtues I am considering, in this course of lectures, temperance and courage certainly could not be ascribed to the Divine Nature, which has neither bodily desires nor pain to endure nor perils to face. It would be equally absurd to ascribe faith or hope to the Omniscient; and these two virtues cannot even be ascribed, I have argued, to Christ as Man by Christian believers; for although he was not omniscient in his human mind, faith in him requires ascription to him of such fullness and clarity of knowledge as excludes his being the subject of either virtue. If we know anything at all of his teaching from the Gospels, he taught with absolute authority, and not as the scribes; he taught as one who saw and knew; knew who and what he was, to what end he was here on Earth, how his earthly life must end, and what joy and glory lay before him.

In regard to this reasoning I may well be accused of ignoring assured results of critical scholarship, confusion about literary forms, and so on. But as a logician I am quite competent to judge the sort of argument I find used by Bible critics; and I judge the arguments to be

very often bad arguments, because where the truth-value of premises and conclusion is known independently of any theological disputes, arguments parallel to the critics' would lead from true premises to a false conclusion.

However, I have no need to go into the bad arguments used by Bible critics; though it needs to be flatly said that they are simply unable to grasp the nature of argument if they suppose that ignorance about their premises ought to stop one from challenging the passage from the premises to a further conclusion. Nor need I discuss how reliable the Gospel accounts of Christ's words actually are; that would be out of place in a philosophical discussion. It is anyhow clear that we know nothing at all about Christ's words except by way of the Gospel record. By that record Christ did claim to teach with absolute certainty and authority. If the records are in this respect unreliable, two things follow.

Firstly: in this case there is a wide gap between the historic figure of Christ and the figure presented in the Gospel: a gap so wide that we could then know only in a theoretical and conjectural way what the actual teaching of Christ was. We should in fact be in the same position as Platonic scholars trying to divine what Socrates actually thought and said. But then for us Christ would be such a figure of theory and conjecture that faith in him would be as much of an absurdity as faith in Socrates; there could be no question of believing his word or following his precepts; for we could have no well-grounded opinion about what he taught or prescribed, if the only clues to this were as untrustworthy as they would be on the present supposition.

Secondly: Let us consider directly what follows if indeed Christ did not claim knowledge and authority in the style reported in the Gospels. We are in that case simply crazy if we stake our lives and souls on our belief in a teaching which he may never have put out at all in the form that has come down to us, and which we are now to suppose was in any case an expression only of what he thought or conjectured, not of what he claimed to know. Obviously our having faith also requires that Christ did really know, not just claim to know; if he were one of the many people who put on airs of authority because they have strong unfounded convictions, then we need pay no special heed to his teaching at all.

Faith in Christ is a pure absurdity unless the believer is convinced that what he himself believes by faith, Christ simply knew; the hope of the Gospel is utterly vain for one who does hold that the Glory he himself only hopes for is something that Christ foresaw with certainty as his own reward and could faithfully promise to his true disciples. So faith and hope in Christ make sense only on a view of him that positively excludes his own possession of these two virtues. And in drawing this conclusion I myself am only saying 'If' like Alice; I have not claimed to prove that faith and hope in Christ are justified, but only that if they are to be justified, a certain thesis about him is a condition *sine qua non*.

The remaining three virtues with which I deal in this book – charity, prudence, and justice – are on the contrary attributes not only of Christ in his human nature but also of the Divine Nature. Justice is a perplexing and multiform concept even as applied to men and human

acts; and though we must ascribe to God both distributive and retributive justice, severe problems arise here. I shall return to these matters in the next chapter but one. In any case, it is part of human justice that a man should be truthful in his statements and faithful to his promises; and these forms or elements of justice must be ascribed without any qualification to God, or else there can be no question of absolute reliance on an alleged Divine revelation.

'Prudence' and 'providence' are in origin two forms of the same Latin word; etymologies are often misleading, this one is not. At the beginning of the Ia IIae Aquinas says that man is shown to be in God's image by possessing free choice and being master of his own acts: the practical wisdom with which men guide their affairs is a faint reflection of the Divine Providence that reaches mightily from end to end of the world and orders all things smoothly; 'remaining in himself,' said Xenophanes, 'he does all things easily by the thought of his mind'. The resemblance between human and Divine practical wisdom has indeed so struck men that they come to think man can and must be his own providence. This thought is not confined to atheists: it infects also the thought of professed Christians. But more of this later.

Prudence and justice then are properly ascribable to God; but this ascription depends on the idea of a created world to be providently planned and justly governed. For charity, or love, it is quite different. Love is just what God is, and is eternally; before the mountains were brought forth or ever the Earth and the world were made; independently of any creatures made or yet to be

made; and of course independently of any creatures con-
templated as mere possibilities never to be realised, since
love towards a person merely dreamed of is a folly confined to men. The wisest of the Greek and Roman pagan
thinkers divined that God is endowed with an eternal
and blessed life independently of the world; for
Christians God's eternal life is a life of love, but this
truth does not annul or make trivial the truth discovered
by the pagans.

Spinoza tells us that he who loves God cannot desire
that God should love him in return. This utterance has
naturally given rise to a great deal of *Schwärmerei*; here
as elsewhere – whatever the general practice of writers
on Spinoza may be – to see what he means to prove we
must look at the proof. In the present case it is not hard
to expound Spinoza's meaning accurately. Spinoza thinks
of love in terms of an access of joy to the lover from
thinking of the beloved; a friend of God will no doubt
have such access of joy when he thinks of God; but the
unchangeable God cannot be supposed to have an access
of joy from thinking anew of his friend; and a change-
able God, I have often argued, is no God. Spinoza goes
on to argue that God's true lover cannot wish it were
otherwise, since so to wish is to wish concerning God that
he were not God. Though they would not use Spinoza's
words, it is quite clear that many Doctors of the Church –
Augustine, Anselm, Aquinas, for example – would fully
accept both his doctrine on this point and his reason
for it.

The contrary doctrine, that God needs created persons
to love or else is not a loving God, can have crept in

among Christians only through ignorance or neglect or misunderstanding of the doctrine of the Trinity. I remember once hearing a pious Roman Catholic lady say that she preferred not to think of the Trinity. It reminds me of the Archdeacon in the story, who was asked what he thought would happen to him when he died, and answered 'I suppose I shall enjoy eternal bliss, but please let us not discuss such a depressing subject.' We may well suppose – and there is nothing uncharitable about this: one cannot be charitable or uncharitable to figures in a story or in logical examples – that the Archdeacon's treasure was on Earth and he was only kidding himself that his heart was elsewhere. But charity forbids me so to judge the lady, who is or was in the real world. Possibly she feared that if she thought about the Trinity she would get into a muddle and jeopardize her faith by running into temptation. Whatever she meant, what she said was appalling: the Blessed Trinity, *res quibus fruendum est* as Augustine said, *the* Things to be enjoyed, the food of men and angels without which they must pine in famine for ever – *that* is something best not thought about! If the good motive I have suggested underlay her words, all the same I fear she erred: she should have had the courage of faith and plunged towards her Lord, like the Apostle for whom I was named, across the deep waters. And I too must take the plunge, unworthy as I am.

I will begin from some considerations in the philosophy of McTaggart. I make bold to say that under God I owe my very self to McTaggart, for it was knowledge of his philosophy that kept alight in me a longing for the

infinite and eternal that was not to be quenched by the noisy winds of the world in the storms of youth. In *Some Dogmas of Religion* McTaggart raises a difficulty about whether a freely creative God can be a person. If God is freely creative, then outside him there exists nothing except what he freely chooses; there are not even possibilities, there is nothing at all. And God could have chosen that there be nothing at all. In that case, McTaggart argues, God would be a solitary person without an Other. Nothing we know of personality gives us any ground to suppose that such personality is even conceivable. We find only persons who are in relation to an Other, an Other existing independently of their choice; and in youth and manhood and old age, in sickness and health, awareness of oneself waxes and wanes with awareness of an Other from which oneself is distinct. A mind for which there is no such Other independent of the will is surely inconceivable. In his lawyerlike way, McTaggart does not claim to have proved his case; but he submits that it is a strong one.

McTaggart's argument about awareness of the Other may fail to strike people because they have some false imagination of God's being confronted by a magazine of possible entities, between which he has to choose. This is an old error, on which I have spoken and written before; I shall not now waste time discussing it; enough to say that the phrase 'the possibility of a rational cephalopod' (for example) can only relate to the same as the phrase 'the possibility of God's making a cephalopod rational', and this in turn is a nominalization of the proposition (be it true or false) 'God can make a

cephalopod rational.' We have to do only with some aspect of God's almighty power, not with some possible but unactual rational cephalopod or with some logical fact that confronts God.

In *The Nature of Existence* McTaggart further argues that a solitary person could not love. Here he is on even firmer ground. One attempt to explain the Christian sense of 'love' or 'charity' goes like this: it appeals to the natural concern each of us feels for himself, just for being the person he is and regardless of all faults; and then the Christian is supposed to extend this sort of concern, I suppose as widely as possible, to other persons just as persons regardless of their faults. (I fear I cannot make much more than this of what C. S. Lewis says about charity in *Mere Christianity*; though he has written much finer things about love elsewhere.) I think this is wrong from beginning to end; and harmfully wrong, because it is bound to lead to humbug, cant, and self-deception. A man's ordinary self-concern is unworthy of the name of love: and if it were love, the man who thinks he is trying to extend that sort of personal interest even to all the other persons he knows will pretty certainly be kidding himself, and will clearly be kidding himself if he thinks he is trying to have that kind of interest in unknown persons.

There is, indeed, as McTaggart pointed out, a special emotional attitude, a kind of wonder, that a lover has towards himself as the bearer of this precious thing, love; McTaggart chose a bad name for it, 'self-reverence' – though the idea of a man's being awed at the birth of love within himself is anyhow better than the idea of

Kant or rather the Serpent (credit where credit is due!) of revering oneself as autonomous promulgator of the moral law. But this awe before one's own love is not love of oneself, and anyhow can arise only from love of another.

These two difficulties – about the need for awareness of an Other, and about the possibility of love in a solitary person – are, however, not difficulties for orthodox Christians: only for others; for Christians falling or fallen away to some form of Monarchianism, for Rabbinical Jews with their traditional reading of '*Adonai elohenu, Adonai echad*', or again for Muslims. In the old language of Church Councils, each of the three Divine Persons *is* an Other to each of the other two Persons: *alius*, someone other, though not *aliud*, another thing. And the Divine Life of the three Persons is nothing else than their eternal mutual love.

Here some will protest that I am equivocating between the normal use of the term 'person' and its technical theological use. I reject the protest. The concept of a person, which we find so familiar in its application to human beings, cannot be clearly and sharply expressed by any word in the vocabulary of Plato or Aristotle; it was wrought with the hammer and anvil of theological disputes about the Trinity and the Person of Christ, and classically formulated by Boethius, who was martyred for the Faith by an Arian emperor. (In the place of his burial Boethius is traditionally venerated as the blessed martyr San Severino by people who have never heard of his writings.) I believe it was the Edinburgh logician Sir William Hamilton who said that a good new term is

like a fortress to dominate country won from the forces of darkness; but those forces never sleep and will strive by their Philological Arm to recover lost territory.

The familiar concept of a person finds linguistic expression not only in the use of a noun for 'person' but also in the use of the personal pronouns 'I, you, he'. And so it is also when we speak of the Divine Persons. Councils of the Church have repeatedly rejected the formula 'He who is the Father is also the Son and the Holy Ghost', while declaring that *what* the Father is – God, Almighty, Omniscient, etc. – the Son and the Holy Ghost also are. As the Preface of the Trinity declares, God the Father with his Son and the Holy Ghost is one Lord and God, but not in the singleness of one Person. And in the Scriptures 'I' and 'you' are used for the discourse of the Divine Persons to one another: 'He shall call to me, Thou art my Father', 'The Lord said to me, Thou art my Son; this day have I begotten thee.' 'Father, glorify me with the glory that I had with thee before the world was.' Where there can be discourse using 'you' and 'I', there can also be mutual love; it would be not less but far more difficult to believe that God could (as a rather bad hymn puts it) live and love alone. (The bad hymn was indeed addressed to the Trinity; but that 'Trinity' is there used *as if* it were the name of a solitary person is just what makes the devotion bad.)

If God is in fact three Persons whose life is mutual love, then that is not the way God happens to be, when it might have been otherwise; it is the way God eternally and necessarily is, even if to our mind the necessity is in this life opaque. Many necessities are opaque to us,

for example the right answers to problems in the theory of numbers. Some ways of presenting natural theology have here had a baneful influence: God, it has been claimed, can be proved by natural reason to be one and absolutely simple; and then there appears no room for the distinction of Persons within the Divinity. But these claims have been in part excessive, in part radically confused.

The radical confusion is to regard the numeral word 'one' as expressing a Divine attribute. This mistake has been decisively exposed by Gottlob Frege; but we need not go into Frege's doctrines to see it is a mistake. A passage in Descartes' *Meditations* exhibits the mistake very clearly. On this point Descartes' teaching is quite standard, if we go by the theological manuals; there is the same mistake in much other writing about God's unity. Descartes is considering an objection that his idea of God comprises various attributes and may have been fadged up by putting together ideas of these attributes, severally derived from a plurality of real beings, not from a single Divine source. He replies 'On the contrary, unity, simplicity, or the inseparability of God's attributes is itself one of the chief perfections I conceive him to have. And at any rate the idea of this one among God's perfections, his unity, could not have been put in me by any cause, without my getting from that cause the idea of other perfections as well; for the cause could not make me understand all the perfections as combined and inseparable without at the same time making me perceive what these perfections were.' I think one need not have read Frege in order to protest that the inseparable going

together of a number of attributes cannot itself be one of the perfections that do go together; we have here, surely, a difference of level; and the appropriateness of Frege's saying just that may now strike us.

Descartes seems to have been uneasy about the matter, since he says that apart from the attributes that do go inseparably together, unity cannot even be conceived. Not but that some men have been insane enough to try to conceive unity, mere unity, as being what God is. But the mind of the Church rejected the Neoplatonic ravings of Eckhart; there is only one God, but God is not The One, God is the Blessed Trinity. And this is not incompatible with the true sense of *'Adonai elohenu, Adonai echad'*, only with the false construction put upon the phrase by the Synagogue: the words are not a declaration that God has this mythical attribute of unity, but a commandment that Israel is to worship the LORD and no other gods.

That there is only one God is in form affirmative, in content negative: numeral terms, Aquinas holds, say nothing positive about the Divinity; *non ponunt aliquid in divinis*. There cannot, as gross paganism represents, be corporeal multiplication of Gods; nor can there, as a subtler paganism would have it, be diverse Divinities with different offices in the world. Something of the subtler paganism has sometimes coloured popular Christian thought about the Three Persons, as if they had different things to do in the creation and government of the world. But the common theological doctrine is that – except for the fact that only one Person became a man, and whatever consequences flow from this – all

external works and deeds of God are common to all the three Persons: grace, for example, is the indwelling of the Father and the Son, as St John's Gospel declares, and not only of the Holy Ghost. It is just on this account, Aquinas teaches, that natural reason, proceeding from effects in the world to God as their cause, can tell us nothing about any distinction of the Persons, and so must be silent on the question whether there is only one Divine Person or rather several (*Summa Theologica* Ia q.32 a.1).

I think it is here significant that after his sublime writing about the nature of the Divine Life Aristotle goes on to say 'Whether this nature is one or many, and how many, is something not to be passed over.' This passage has given scandal to some, and has led to suppositions about strata of composition, evolutionary stages of Aristotle's thought. A Christian cannot indeed follow Aristotle in holding that the number of everlastingly moved heavenly spheres manifests the number of everlasting Divine Beings; but he must hold Aristotle to have been right in not *a priori* excluding plurality from the Divine, and even right in holding that this plurality is somehow manifested in the world: once we know (which a Christian must say we can know only by revelation) the number of Divine Persons and the order in which they stand, we can see by hindsight what created structures mirror this eternal order. In the very same chapter of the *Metaphysics*, after mentioning the plurality of eternal unmoved movers, Aristotle insists that there can be but one eternal first mover, that this nature is not materially multipliable like human nature.

Here, in conjecturing that there may be many eternal movers who yet share one unmultipliable Divine Nature and Life, Aristotle reached the very frontier of human reason concerning God; and for a Christian the contradiction in which Aristotle is here involved is only apparent.

I repeat: God is Love because, and only because, the Three Persons eternally love each other. It is false that God would have been Love all the same if he had been one solitary person everlastingly loving himself; reason could not show us that such a God is even possible, and revelation shows that God is not a solitary self-lover, and therefore could not possibly be such. It is, as I have emphasized, still more false to make God's eternal Love depend upon an eternal need to *create* beings to love and be loved by; much as a lonely human person lacking the company and friendship of fellow-men, will lavish affection on cats or dogs and crowd the house with them.

It was indeed not to Christians for the first time, but to the House of Israel that God was revealed as a God of Love, a God who called in return for our love to him and to our fellows. Christians are much too ready to ignore the fact that the two great commandments of love are the two great commandments *of the Torah*. But God's special love for Israel, a Christian must say, comes because in God's predestination the Messiah, the Son of God, was to be born of that House; that is why 'Israel is my Son, my Firstborn' as Moses declared, in God's name, to Pharaoh. It is conventional, and I think right, to take the prodigal son and his elder brother in the parable as respectively representing the Gentiles and

80

Israel; but let us then not forget that God says for ever-more to Israel in the Person of Christ 'My Son, thou art always with me, and all that I have is thine.' No grace given to the Gentiles can annul that prerogative of Israel nor ever put Gentiles on an equality with Israel.

If this is what we have to say about God's charity towards Israel and towards all men – that he loves us for the sake of his Son, who is our Brother as man – then it is clear what we must say of charity as a human virtue. The primary object of man's charity is not man but God. God is to be loved wholly and above all things; not so our neighbour. The love enjoined in the Torah is clearly God-centred; I have heard of a preacher in our day saying that Christianity ought to be a man-centred, not a God-centred, religion, and no doubt some rabbis preach that way as well, but in either case it is apostasy. A well-known Bible text (1 John iv.20) is of no weight to the contrary; for its application to prove that men should come first in our love is perverse. If a man hates his neighbours whom he has seen, this destroys his claim to love God whom he has not seen; but this is simply the order of inference. In the order of being, love of God comes first, and of its nature overflows into love of our fellow men, who are brothers of God's Son; love of men that does not flow from love of God may be an agreeable thing enough, but it is only part of the fashion of this world that passes away, and we should not overvalue it.

'A God who demands that love of himself shall come first,' I may be told, 'would just be a monster of selfish-ness – even if, as in your story, it is egoism *à trois*.' I reply, in the spirit of what C. S. Lewis says in *The*

Problem of Pain, that it is alike absurd to call God unselfish or to call him selfish. God is not selfish in regard
to his creatures, for they can give him nothing he lacks
or needs and there is no question of his exploiting them;
whatever good they have comes from God as an utterly
free gift that cannot be repaid. But it is equally absurd
to commend God for the sort of unselfishness we commend in good parents. Parents must not allow their
children to grow up unable to seek or find any happiness
except with their parents at home. But God cannot give
his creatures this autonomy. God is the only source, the
only possible source, of love and joy and wisdom; he
cannot give his creatures a happiness that does not derive
from himself, that does not consist in relation to himself.
The Scriptures call God jealous because he demands of
us absolute fidelity and devotion to himself, comparing
God to a husband who will not put up with only
moderate chastity in his wife. But the jealousy of the true
God is not like the envy of human prosperity that sometimes in Greek myth is ascribed to Zeus; God wants us
to be supremely and everlastingly happy; but from our
nature, not by arbitrary decree, we can be happy for ever
only if we love God above all things.

Unselfishness not only is not a virtue ascribable to
God; it just is not a virtue. Self-regarding action may be
virtuous: for example, it is likely to be virtuous to expand
one's own capacities of knowledge and appreciation even
when the chance of using these capacities for the direct
benefit of one's fellows appears slight. Contrariwise,
unselfish, self-sacrificing action is often vicious. People
have shown the greatest neglect of self, endurance of

sufferings, heroism in face of death, in the vilest of causes: like the young Nazi bleeding to death at the post of duty, his duty being the machine-gunning of helpless refugees. I have heard one who professed and called himself Christian refer to Nazism as 'a valid, though limited, experience of solidarity' (or he may have said 'community' or 'relationship'; it was one of these words), and he would no doubt think me very uncharitable to refuse to recognise in this 'valid experience', even in its most heroic manifestations, the spirit of God's Love. St Paul clearly thought otherwise: that one could lack charity even if one gave all one's goods to feed the poor and offered one's body to be burned.

Not any love of others, not any devotion to others, is even good, let alone identifiable with the charity of God. Devotion to a cause is often mere wickedness, and the degree to which the devotee is prepared to sacrifice himself and endure suffering is merely an index of the hellish intensity of his malice. Devotion to an individual, too, can be mere filth and poison; a little experience of life is enough to show cases of a mutual love that is a living death; two people clawing and rending each other, like two cats whom a cruel boy has tied by the tails together and hung over a clothes line.

Even when love is good, it need not be the charity that comes from God and unites us to God for ever. All good comes from God, but not all good is God's grace. The contrapositive, as the logicians say, of the proposition that all good in man is the working of God's grace is the equivalent proposition that all in man that is not the working of God's grace is *not* good: and this is the false

thesis of total depravity. No creature even in Hell can exist totally deprived of good; and whatever good a creature has comes from God. It is another question whether there is in a creature that love of God which alone can bring perfect and everlasting happiness. Earthly love may be good in its season, like the grass and the flowers; but the grass withereth, and the flower fadeth; the world passes away, and the desires of the world; only he who does the will of God shall abide in God's house for ever.

If charity is not to be recognised in men merely from the manifestation of love, however devoted and sacrificial, still less is it to be recognised in some of the things that the Philological Arm has succeeded in making us call charity: these are not just to be depreciated as merely limited goods; they are not good at all. The word 'charity' has associations with ostentatious appearances on subscription lists, with the Charity Organisation Society (think of organising the fire of the Holy Ghost!), with a Lady Bountiful who steals a goose by exorbitant rents and skimped wages and puts down a feather by sending broken victuals around to the cottagers. Still worse, the word is often applied to a fatuous complacency towards every vagary of misconduct and misbelief: the professed Christian who commended the solidarity or whatever it was of the Nazis would often be said to be judging them 'charitably'. I have heard people ascribing to George Lansbury's sanctity the odd impression he had, based on personal contact with Hitler, that the fellow meant well and desired peace. In past history real Saints have had a lot

to do with villainous rulers, and have not been thus deceived by them.

If neither love however intense, however sacrificial, nor yet what we have thus come to call charity, is reliable sign of the charity of God shed abroad in our hearts, then what can be the criterion? It is commonly held by theologians that there is no absolute criterion by which we can judge; the absence of God's love may plainly show, but its presence cannot show forth so plainly that we can be infallibly certain. Nor is it our business so to judge others. But each of us as regards himself may ask a searching question, suggested by an article of the *Summa Theologica* (IaIIae q.119 a.8): Is my heart so fixed upon God that I should not be willing to be separated from him to win any good or to avoid any evil? The form of the question itself excludes a confident affirmative answer based on some sort of introspection; but my true answer had better be Yes, or else there is no charity in me and I am worthless in God's eyes.

Charity towards God presupposes that the mind is directed towards the true God not towards some false idol. Of this element of intentionality I have spoken already in the lecture on Faith. How explicit a conception of God is needed in order to love him truly, in order that love be not misdirected like my senile voter's devotion to 'Mr Macmillan' or my romantic lover's devotion to his fantastically conceived Dulcinea? Such questions are beyond man's power to answer. We can know in a general way that some men remain alienated from the life of God by the ignorance that is in them;

85

our business is not to try to see who stands on which side of the line, but to labour for the removal of ignorance and error; and if we are slack and careless about this, how can we hope to answer in the affirmative the conditional question I culled from Aquinas? On the other hand, it may be that someone who has sought with a pure heart for the knowledge of truth, or the promotion of justice and mercy, will meet with the blessing of the God who is Truth and Justice and Mercy, even though in this life he has had no clear conception of God. We do not know, and it is not our affair: *Quid ad te? Tu me sequere!* It is all in God's hands; and as his Majesty is, so is his Mercy.

For God's sake we must have charity towards our fellow-men: and that means actual love of people individually, not just generalized attitudes of goodwill. We cannot in this life love very many individual people: let us love where we can, and not let love die in indifference and oblivion or be extinguished in a quarrel. Let us above all root out day by day from our hearts the weeds of envy, anger, and malice that continually spring up, before they develop into firm-rooted flourishing hatreds. If we cannot love our enemies actively, let us at least forgive them, since each of us stands in such need of forgiveness. Let us be generous in judging the motives and meanings of other men; this is not a matter of preferring love to truth – nothing blinds the heart more than malice; and contrariwise a disposition to construe one's neighbour's words as meaning something true or reasonable pays off in increased mutual understanding. Let us do good where we can and do wrong to none. If

so we live we may hope by God's mercy to come to that Glory in which all men love and all are lovable, and where without care or fret there is infinite leisure to get to know those who will be our friends for ever because both we and they were God's friends first.

5

PRUDENCE

I am here concerned with the virtue of *phronēsis* or practical wisdom, which the medievals called *prudentia*. And my first question is: How far is the virtue of prudence, or practical wisdom, a matter of observing laws? And are laws meant just as rough guides to conduct, or as laws always to be kept, never to be transgressed?

I shall defend the doctrine of there being moral precepts that are never to be broken. This doctrine is often now stigmatised as legalism: if so, then I count myself a legalist. One argument often used against legalism is a gross confusion. Legalism is a doctrine about an allegedly necessary, not allegedly sufficient, condition for the good life. To borrow an apt metaphor from Thomas Hobbes, I might say that the King has fenced the roads not to stop travellers in their journey but to keep them in the way. If you are in the King's highway, that does not show that your journey is really necessary or well-advised or that you are not going in the diametrically wrong direction. But you go off the highway, to take as you hope a short cut, at your own peril. You have no map of the open country, and in it there are many perils for the reckless traveller: precipices, bogs, barren wastes, trackless forests, wild beasts, and

the castles of robber barons. If you are lost by your own folly, in spite of the King's warnings, he may send a rescue party, but he has not promised to do so.

In one way the metaphor of hedges fails. It suggests that it is always clear when we are breaking through the hedge and transgressing; and of course that is not so. Any terms in which we can state and grasp laws relating to conduct will be words without a sharp boundary in their application. Frege was no doubt right in requiring sharp boundaries for logical and mathematical terms; all the same, to expect that we can use only sharply delimited terms in law and morals is, as Aristotle said, a sign of a lack of good education. Is this a case of killing someone or just a case of not taking special care to keep someone alive? Is this form of words a falsehood or is it just equivocal? It is folly to expect a definite right answer to all such questions; and this must mitigate the rigour in application of any law forbidding the killing of the innocent or the utterance of lies. But from this people will infer that exceptions can be made to a law where it is not at all doubtful how the law should apply; where it is merely going to lead to horribly bad consequences if we apply it. This inference is clearly faulty. Naaman may have been innocent of apostasy from the God of Israel whom alone he had vowed to worship when he bowed in the temple of Rimmon with his king; this is because the meaning of Naaman's act is diversely construable; it does not follow that there are not acts that unequivocally signify idolatry of a false god, nor does it follow that such acts are permissible merely because the man is tempted to

apostasy by a threat that otherwise he, and his, will be thrown into a burning fiery furnace.

One argument against legalism is that one should be guided not by law but by love: *ama et fac quod vis*. But I argued in the last chapter that not any love is charity; and having had some feelings of love, in some sense of that very ambiguous word, when you acted is no criterion at all of your having acted out of charity. Love is anyhow not just externally related to the expression of love. In the film *Oklahoma*, it is said in a song about a dead man that he loved his fellow-men but he never let it show. Now of course it would make sense to say of some brave soldier that though in the campaign he was often suffering pain, terror, and fatigue, he never let it show. Love of your fellow-men is not like pain, terror, and fatigue; it is not a feeling that may or may not come out in the conduct of the man who feels it. If you act a certain way you may show you were not acting out of charity, regardless of how you feel inside.

The sense in which I wish to take such sayings as *Ama et fac quod vis* or 'Love is the fulfilment of the Law' is not that if you have enough of a certain feeling you can do what you like, it counts as, or is as good as, the fulfilment of the Law: but rather, that if you have charity, and in proportion as that charity is perfect, you will in fact do what by publicly available criteria just *is* a fulfilment of the Law. I may add that the question 'What would be the really loving thing to do?' is as unclear as the question 'What in my case would Jesus do?', which some English children were taught to ask themselves. It is for example not at all likely – whatever

Prudence

Bishop John Robinson may think – to help a young man to decide whether to get bedded down with his girl. And St Thomas More might well by this standard be judged unloving in sacrificing his own and his family's fortune, and finally his own life, to a scruple about telling a lie that his King wished him to tell. But it does not take Catholic faith for men to find More's resistance noble.

A more serious enemy of legalism is consequentialism: the doctrine that we ought to try to reckon the consequences, as far ahead as we can, of the various alternative actions, and choose the best one. A particular form of consequentialism is utilitarianism: here, the optimific alternative is supposed to be the one that brings about the greatest benefit or the greatest happiness *of the greatest number*. Difficulties of measuring benefit or happiness are often raised: but utilitarianism can be shot down without going into these.

A realization how inane is the phrase 'the greatest happiness of the greatest number' does not come, to my mind, either from doubt regarding the measure of happiness or from any objection to happiness as specifying the end. Such thoughts are not needed; the radical difficulty arises from the double superlative, if it is taken seriously and not just as a piece of piling-up rhetoric like Churchill's 'Never was so much owed by so many to so few'. I should hate to pick Churchill's sentence to pieces; it was not logic but rhetoric, which very effectively conveyed a sense of enormous obligation, and is not to be judged by working out the logical purport of the multiple comparisons involved; a greater

debt than ever before, owed by more people, owed to fewer people. But such multiple comparisons can have surprising and unintended consequences: as was pointed out by H. W. Fowler, under the apt heading 'Illogicalities', in *Modern English Usage*. (In honour of his memory, I will say that though he had no formal training in logic Fowler often showed a keen eye or nose for such logical points.)

Fowler's example involved two comparatives: it was in effect 'Never were finer lines perverted to a meaner use', the implied 'than' phrase being of course 'than *these* fine lines', the ones the author of the example was referring to. Fowler points out that the double comparative, far from strengthening the logical force of what is said, weakens it. Of the three propositions: 'Never were lines perverted to a meaner use than these fine lines', 'Never were fine lines perverted to a meaner use than these fine lines', 'Never were finer lines perverted to a meaner use than these fine lines', each in succession is not logically stronger but logically weaker: the first is a generalisation relating to all lines, the second relates only to all fine lines, and the third relates only to all lines finer than the fine lines the author of the dictum had in mind. This should be obvious enough when spelled out, and it just shows how easily our first impression about the logical force of double comparisons may mislead us.

Let us now turn to an example closer to 'the greatest happiness of the greatest number'. Suppose it is alleged that Professor Pfefferkorn has read more books in more languages than any other German professor. If we work

this out, Professor Pfefferkorn's scholarship is less impressive than it at first sounds. For consider what it implies if we compare Pfefferkorn's scholarship with that of some rival, say Nussbaum. Does our proposition imply that Pfefferkorn must have read more books, in more languages, that Nussbaum? No, in fact what it implies is that the number of languages in which *Pfefferkorn* has read more books than any other German professor is greater than the number of languages in which *Nussbaum* has read more books than any other German professor: and the like must hold if we here replace Nussbaum's name by the name of any other rival of Pfefferkorn. But now what is said about the extent of Pfefferkorn's reading turns out to be quite modest. Pfefferkorn can score a language as being one in which he has read more books than any other German professor if it is e.g. an exotic language in which he has read only a few books, but more than any other German professor has read *in that language*. And in this way Pfefferkorn can win the competition on the terms stated although Nussbaum is a vastly more learned man than Pfefferkorn in the fewer but more important languages that both professors know.

Similarly for our case. To say that an alternative A will secure more happiness for more people than any other alternative, say B, is to say that the number of people whom alternative A would make happier than any alternative other than A would make them is greater than the number of people whom alternative B would make happier than any alternative other than B would make them. This is not quite easy to take in,

but if we work it out we readily see that the felicific quality of alternative A may be as little impressive as the learning of Professor Pfefferkorn; and why then go all out to secure alternative A?

I imagine that the immense appeal of 'the greatest happiness of the greatest number' is that it arouses a feeling of concern for the broad masses rather than some privileged class. 'When wilt thou save the people/Lord, in thy mercy, when?/The people, Lord, the people/Not crowns or thrones but men.' If you reject the slogan, you write yourself down an élitist. But 'élitist' and 'elect' are connected, not only in etymology: and a lot of the Judaeo-Christian revelation is about God's election. 'You only have I known of all the nations upon Earth.' 'I pray not for the world, but for those whom thou hast given me out of the world.' There appears good reason to believe that God does not design the greatest happiness – if this means the Beatific Vision – for the greatest number. That happiness is indeed what men are for: without it they fail irretrievably. But the teleology of an acorn similarly points to its growing into an oak; and most acorns do not. This, as I said before, does not mean that as regards those acorns which do not the Maker has been bungling or wasteful.

In the present dispensation I can see no reason to doubt St Thomas's words: *pauciores qui salvantur*, it is the smaller number who are being saved. He was after all only echoing the severe warning of his Master about the narrow gate to life and the broad road to destruction. It may not always be so. Many Christians have hoped for

a Messianic kingdom on Earth before the final consummation: one in which, though death the last enemy has not been overcome, sin lies crushed. In such a world, where evil rulers and perverse laws and corrupting mass media and oppression of the poor had been done away for ever, nightmares of the past never to return and trouble men, those who grew up to mortal life would predominantly be saved. About this I cannot now argue. For now, the world lies in wickedness, and only those who by deliberate choice swim against the current can hope to be saved. A God who so orders things is not concerned for anything that may be called the greatest happiness of the greatest number, so far as these generations of men are concerned.

Objections to what I have said are likely to take the form of protests that such dispensations of Providence as I suppose would be unjust or cruel rather than that they would be foolish or improvident; so perhaps I may leave them aside till I come to the question of Divine justice in the next chapter. But I have gone into this matter here because there has existed what may be called theistic rule-utilitarianism, e.g. in Berkeley and Paley the doctrine that, through our limited wisdom and foresight, means that we must not calculate for the best possible consequences, God can and does make such calculations, and his commands are to be justified as setting up practices that will lead to the greatest happiness of the greatest number of his rational creatures. For this doctrine I can see no warrant; but I shall go into the matter a little more, since it is worth while to see just what is wrong with theistic rule-utilitarianism.

In one sense indeed we cannot imagine God to be bound by law: we cannot suppose that independently of God in some supercelestial place (*en hyperouraniōi topōi*) there just *is* some paradigm of the Good, to which God like ourselves is bound to conform. But this thought, although important, is irrelevant to the question whether God can be absolutely trusted to act in certain ways and not to act in certain other ways. In particular: can we be absolutely certain that God is truthful in his revelation and faithful to his promises? I shall argue that on the doctrine of the theistic rule-utilitarians we could have no such certainty. On that doctrine, the reason why men are absolutely bound – for example – to abstain from lying is that men are too ignorant of the overall picture of things to judge when exceptions can be made. But why should not God judge that a false revelation will work out for men's good? On theistic rule-utilitarian principles, I cannot see any reason to rule out this suggestion; but in that case Christian faith simply crumbles away.

This argument is of course an *ad hominem* argument, addressed to those theistic rule-utilitarians who would profess themselves Christians (and I know of no others). In admitting that the argument is *ad hominem* I am not with bare face putting over a fallacy. It is just a vulgar error to imagine that an *ad hominem* argument is as such fallacious; the deduction by A from B's premises of a conclusion B cannot consistently accept is a fair procedure, rather than an eristic sleight of hand, provided that A uses valid inferential methods; the result may be unpleasant to B, but if B is shown by valid argu-

ment that his present corpus of beliefs needs correction, then this is clear gain for B, if only B will accept it, and not just victory for A.

But I am afraid the result with *this* B, the present-day theistic rule-utilitarian, might be that he dropped from his corpus of beliefs, not the doctrine that God need keep no rules because he can see without rules what is best in each set of conditions, but rather the doctrine that God always reveals the truth and always keeps his promises.

This is not just imagination on my part of what *might* be concluded. There are many nowadays who hold that God's revelation is to be found in several 'great' religions, each of which is for those who practise it the ordinary way of salvation; such people of course do not think that God reveals only the truth. Similarly, some people do not believe that God can be trusted to keep his promises, for they think he has already renegued on his promises to Israel; and by expressing fear that man may exterminate himself in war, or a tyrant come to world power and destroy the Christian religion, they show that they don't take God's promises to the Church any more seriously than his promises to Israel.

Theistic rule-utilitarianism is in fact an inherently unstable position. In the Judaeo-Christian tradition, and by inheritance from this in Islam too, there is the notion of apostasy as something absolutely excluded: the believer may not deny the truth and must not count the cost of refusing to apostatize to himself or to his nearest and dearest; he must leave that to God. But if you are prepared to believe that God himself is not bound by a

rule of truthfulness, and indeed has revealed falsehoods as the ordinary means of salvation to the mass of men, then you are not going to face much sooner than profess those falsehoods if it comes to the crunch. What is called an ecumenical spirit about the varieties of human religion in fact goes with depreciation of the glory of martyrdom. But I shall have more to say about that when I come on to the virtue of courage.

In any event I can take a shorter way with theistic rule-utilitarianism, and need not confine myself to embarrassing *ad hominem* arguments against professed Christians who have held this position. The whole idea of God's working for the best possible outcome is incoherent. However good and happy we were, we could be better and happier, since the good enjoyed by a creature is only limited; and there could be more of us. The idea of an absolutely best possible world, or an absolutely best possible state of affairs, is merely incoherent, like the idea of a biggest natural number. (This insight, like much else, I owe to McTaggart.) So we may dismiss the Leibnizian dream of a heap of possible worlds out of which God picks the best of all; and equally we may dismiss any charge made against God that this world is *not* the best possible.

The incoherence of this notion, and again the incoherence of the double comparison involved in the double superlative 'the greatest happiness of the greatest number', does not suffice to show that the idea of a man's going for that alternative available for him which has the best possible consequences supplies no sort of coherent guide for human action. But though I have not

established this yet, I believe it to be true, and I shall now argue for it.

One argument against the coherence of this policy, an argument that has always seemed to me decisive, is to be found in Arthur Prior's article 'The Consequences of Actions'. How are we to specify the consequences of an alternative course of action open to A at time t? We may pose a dilemma here, arguing first from an indeterministic view of human actions, then from a deterministic one. If we hold an indeterministic view, then we see pretty quickly that there is no such thing for A at time t as a review of consequences for the various alternatives open to him in order to pick out the best alternative. For A's act, whichever it is, will place other free agents B, C, D, . . . in positions of choice which would not have arisen but for A's act; and then, on the indeterministic view, A cannot fully foresee how B and C and D will choose, and therefore cannot fully foresee how the consequences of any alternative he himself chooses will work out.

This is a rather abstract argument, so I shall illustrate the extremely unforeseeable character of human affairs on the indeterministic view. Consider Brutus deliberating whether to take part in the conspiracy to murder Caesar, to abstain but keep silent, or to denounce the plot to Caesar. Brutus could not foresee even the most immediate consequences of any alternative; how Cassius, Caesar, Cicero, Mark Antony would react; and if he considered the matter of remote consequences at all, he might reflect that these would reverberate to the end of time; this he could see in a general way, but of course

he could not possibly foresee the play Shakespeare was going to write, the heroism and villainy of the French revolutionaries inspired by his act, and so on indefinitely.

Let me take a more familiar and down-to-earth example: a young man wondering whether to seek a girl's hand in marriage. The only thing prudence can here dictate is that the girl be (as Victorians would say) eligible; he need not expect God to let him off the consequences if he marries a hopeless fool, a shrew, or a wanton. But there can be no question of going after the best possible choice. Is he to look round the young ladies of his acquaintance and decide to pursue the *most* eligible? He cannot of course foresee if she will accept him; nor can he foresee what their fortune together will be if they do marry. He cannot tell whether they will have children – childbearing can of course be prevented, but it cannot be guaranteed – nor what their children will be like. And if he decides not to marry or not to have children, he cannot rationally judge that this is the best possible alternative; he cannot in principle know the value of what he has thus forgone.

It is sometimes argued in this connexion that one can ignore the consequences of an action after a certain time because they die out like ripples on a pond. The examples I have given are enough to refute this. The choice made by Brutus still has many consequences, after two thousand years, and human acts of generation are equally enduring in their consequences. When a British Princess marries a commoner, the heralds finds some line of royal descent for him from a King of England; and they need not be cheating. I imagine we may truly say of some

sufficiently remote King, as Charles II said of himself, that he is the father of his people, or at least a good many of them; and that means that but for the generative acts of some long-dead King many of the present population of Britain would not be there.

Are things any better for the 'best available alternative' ethic if we go over to determinism? They are not. Determinism could at best tell us that the consequences I have called unforeseeable are 'in principle' foreseeable, it could not enable us any better to foresee them. And apart from that there are difficulties raised for the very idea of choosing between alternatives if determinism is true.

It would indeed be too cheap and easy an argument to say that if determinism is true there just are no alternatives; what determinism implies, as I see it, is rather that if there are to be alternative actions at time t, then before t there must be assumed corresponding alternative courses of history that would lead up to one choice or another. Now, on any view, a human being is a very complicated and unstable organism, and a minute difference of stimulus may produce dramatic differences of response; the hoary old example of this is the difference between a telegram 'OUR SON KILLED IN CRASH' and one reading 'YOUR SON KILLED IN CRASH'. So a very small rewriting of the world's history up to time t might be enough, on a deterministic view, to give a different choice of action at t.

That is not the difficulty, then: that determinism must exclude there being alternatives. The inescapable difficulty, I should say, is that this now rules out the agent's having the kind of foresight that would enable him to make a rational choice of the best alternative. For the (perhaps

only minutely) different pasts that would issue in different present choices at time *t* are not surveyable by the agent himself; and they may well have different effects after time *t*, quite apart from producing different choices at *t*, and these further effects the agent will be quite unable to work out. Anyhow, the agent clearly cannot deliberate whether to have had one past rather than another; he might as well (in Aristotle's words) deliberate about whether Troy shall have fallen.

This again is a rather abstract argument, and I shall put flesh on its bones by citing one example that was invented by Martin Gardner and published in the *Scientific American*. (It doesn't matter if I have changed it a little, because the form I shall give is that one that suits my purposes.) A young man has just finished the university course leading to his first degree, and has been exceptionally successful both academically and athletically. He has to choose between an academic and an athletic career. His deliberation is guided by the fact that his paternity is doubtful; he doesn't know whether he is really the son of his mother's husband or of her lover, and she is equally uncertain. If he is the son of his putative father, then he has a considerable chance of having inherited a rare congenital condition of the central nervous system, which leads to precocious mental development followed by rapid and incurable degeneration and death. On the other hand, no professional athlete has ever been known to develop this disease. The young man therefore decides to be a professional athlete; by his making this choice, he reasons, it will become overwhelmingly probable that he is the son of his mother's

lover and not of her husband and has therefore not inherited this lethal gene from his father.

There may be those who think the young man's deliberations make sense; to me, as to Martin Gardner himself, they appear merely crazy. He is already son of the one man or already son of the other man, and he can no more do anything about that or sensibly deliberate about it than about the fall of Troy. A determinist might indeed think that the supposed statistics about athletes not contracting the disease are to be explained by the theory that possession of the lethal gene overwhelmingly disposes a man not to choose an athletic but an intellectual career; I am not here and now arguing about that point, I am only saying that it is not a point the young man himself can rationally take into account in practical reasoning. And this is the special instance of my general thesis: if we assume a deterministic view of choice, there will be cause-factors of an agent's choices that his own deliberations will have to ignore, even though he cannot assume them to be barren of future consequences other than such as fructify through his own choice; and this makes it impossible for him so to forecast alternative futures as to know which is optimific.

So far I have left unchallenged the ground assumption that we can in principle list the exclusive and exhaustive set of alternative actions open to an agent at time t. But in fact this ought to be challenged. When I delivered this chapter as a lecture in Cambridge I merely expressed the doubt in an intuitive way; but Lars Bergström has since kindly given me his *Noûs* paper 'Utilitarianism and Alternative Actions', in which the conclusion is

drawn, with equal logical rigour and intuitive clarity, that no *unique* exclusive and exhaustive set of alternatives for an agent at time *t* can in general be specified at all. Bergström does not himself draw from what I venture to call his discovery what seems to me the manifest conclusion, that it is all up with utilitarianism: but I think one ought to.

People might suppose that though utilitarianism is no good as an ethical theory of individual action it is still the theory to apply for large-scale planning, in which individuals need not figure. Even though individual generative actions make a difference to who is around a hundred years hence, it might be argued that statistical considerations are enough to show what sort of gene pool there will then be; and it is just such generic forecasts, surely, that we both need and can get for optimific large-scale and long-term planning.

I think such planning, now so fashionable, is a mere pipe-dream. I shall not even need Bergström's point about alternatives to bring out this result; though of course the point is just as forceful here. Nor need I insist on the gross fallibility of such predictions in actual experience. There is a further theoretical reason why such predictions, large-scale and long-term, must be grossly fallible, and why the progress of science and technology, so far from improving matters, makes the prospects for such forecasting bleak indeed.

Necessarily we can in principle make forecasts only on the basis of the scientific knowledge that we have, not on the basis of scientific discoveries yet to be made. But presumably there will be more and more scientific dis-

coveries made: *plurimi pertransibunt et multiplex erit scientia*; 'many will run to and fro and knowledge will be increased'. We cannot forecast these discoveries, nor the technology that will flow from them, nor the difference to the life of our great-grandchildren that the new technology will make. Just imagine somebody, before the discoveries of Faraday and Oersted, or again of Mme Curie, trying to forecast the world of the future on the basis of the science then available! And the faster science and technology progress, the huger is the unpredictable element. Let me emphasize that I am not here talking about unpredictability in principle or presuming that the case against determinism is decisive; I am talking about large-scale long-term planning as a guide to the actions of men with our capacities, and arguing that such a guide must by the nature of the case be blind.

I would make two more brief remarks in this connexion. First, there comes out here once more what has often been remarked, the extreme epistemic difference between our apprehensions of the future and of the past. New science and technology do indeed require us to keep revising and amplifying our chronicle of the human past, but not to nearly so great an extent as they upset our estimate of the future.

Secondly, people may suppose that what we cannot do with our own brains in the way of large-scale long-term forecasts, computers with their superior minds can do for us. This is mere superstition, and on the part of some people it must be deception, even if it is also self-deception. If the brain is a computer, it is a computer much more complex than any man-made computer, with powers

(including powers of recovery of function after damage) which no man-made computer remotely approaches; and honest workers in computer science often frankly admit this. Years ago it was predicted that some years before 1975 the world's chess champion would be a computer; the prophecy has been falsified, and this ought to have put paid to the absurd pretence that the computers we have now made are our intellectual superiors. Of course I deny that they think at all, but I need not now insist on that; anyhow they simply do not think better than we.

A physiologist colleague of mine at Leeds was amused to receive a letter from a kind-hearted lady asking whether he could not abandon his cruel animal experiments in favour of getting a computer to tell him what the results of the experiments would be. But the reverence this shows for computers as the dwelling-place of minds superior to ours is to my mind sinister, not just laughable: it is idolatry and consultation of oracles revived; and men may soon, if they are not doing so already, be asking their idols whom to kill. 'Let them that make them be made like to them: and all those who put their trust in them.'

I therefore reject consequentialism, root and branch; but of course that does not mean I think an act has to be appraised regardless of what it brings about. What it means is that in such a series of act-descriptions as you find in Elizabeth Anscombe's *Intention* and other people's writings – moving an arm up and down, moving a pump-lever, making a rather squeaky noise, pumping water, pumping poisoned water, poisoning the inhabit-

ants of a house, etc., etc. – the man of prudence, *phronēsis*, will apply a cut-off procedure, after which he ceases to consider *further* descriptions of the action in terms of its effects. And legalism will further hold that if in working out the description of an action we reach certain descriptions, e.g. that it is an act of blasphemy, or killing the innocent, or perversion of just judgment, or perjury, or adultery; then we need consider no further: this is already the cut-off point and the act is ruled out.

The idea that applying a cut-off procedure can be prudential is not one we ought to suspect. Consider a life-insurance company: it will collect relevant information about a man's health and occupation; but only up to a certain point. And as regards the specific legalistic cut-off points in deliberations, there will often be a secular justification for these, such as Moore gives in *Principia Ethica* (though this leads to a certain inconsistency, which he does not notice, in his view of what we ought to do). Namely: There are certain simple, straightforward, rules which reason can show not only deserve to be generally observed, but also are such as we generally ought not even to think of violating. So much we can plainly see; but our ignorance of present circumstances and future contingencies, and our propensity to load the scale of judgment in favour of ourselves and those we care about, will never allow us to see clearly that an exception might be made; so, Moore concludes, an exception indeed never ought to be made.

Moore's argument is rational, and stands on its own feet; but it may prove insufficient, in circumstances of

severe temptation, as a means of persuading oneself to keep the rule. And it was for this purpose, of showing reasons that would do more for a man against temptation than Moore's argument, that I developed the considerations found in the last essay of *God and the Soul*. Moore's argument, it might be said, certainly shows that departure from the rules must be very risky; but must we not sometimes take risks, and may not taking risks sometimes turn out in the event to have been justified? It was to answer this consideration, not in order to show the desirability of keeping the rules, that I appealed to considerations about God's Providence.

If there is an all-embracing Providence, this thought can give us great confidence as well as great fear. We may then be confident that the rules of prudence are a promulgation to our mind of God's Law, a reflection in our mind of God's Providence; and we need not worry that by keeping God's Law we could by misadventure get the world into a mess; 'I did not make the world, and he who made it will guide.' On the other hand, a real assent to the doctrine of God's all-encompassing knowledge and power may overawe us to the extent that we banish even the vain wish to secure some good or avoid some evil, for ourselves or for those we care for, by defiance of God's Law. And this, I think, is the fear of the Lord that is the beginning of wisdom.

We are to eschew evil, of various sorts that can readily be discerned; and we are to do good, without a wild-goose chase after the best. We fail of course even in this; but it is only about our failures that we have to worry, not about the long-term results of our actions. 'Therefore

do not be anxious for tomorrow, for tomorrow will be anxious for itself. Let the day's own trouble be sufficient for the day. . . . Therefore do not be anxious, saying "What shall we eat?" or "What shall we drink?" or "What shall we wear?" For the Gentiles seek all these things, and your Heavenly Father knows that you need them all. But seek first his Kingdom and his Justice, and all these things shall be yours as well.' Many of the world's troubles arise because we give a false prudence priority over justice. But what justice consists in is the topic of the next chapter; I am afraid I can give only a partial answer.

6

JUSTICE

Justice, as I have said, is one of the attributes of God; and man's justice is to be understood as an image, however distorted, of God's Justice, even as man's prudence or practical wisdom is an image of Divine Providence. In the bliss of the Trinity, before all worlds, there is no place for justice, only for love; justice applies to God only as Ruler of the world; not even to God as Creator, for there can be no question of rights and wrongs in regard to creation. But justice has always been seen by men as something they desperately need and are always cheated of: to this need both the appeal to Divine Justice and the communist faith in a future just society bear witness, even though the two parties each hold of the other, and a cynic might hold of both, that to hope justice is to be got that way is wishful thinking.

Justice is an immensely problematic concept: there are, in old jargon, many parts of justice – there are many strands plaited together, and each strand carries many knotty problems. In one chapter I can cover only a little ground. I begin with veracity and fidelity: telling the truth and keeping promises. I have said that veracity and fidelity must be ascribed to God without any qualification: God's word is truth, and God's promises are sure. A Christian, if he thinks, consequently, cannot yield a fraction on these points; for to do so would

destroy the foundation of his faith and hope. All the same, he must take a hard look at the doubts from the side of moral philosophy which, if well grounded, would show that God's absolute truthfulness and fidelity could be called in question.

A distinction must be drawn between lying and the breaking of promises. Lying, I shall argue, is always wicked, even for men; that God should put forth a lie, or make his lies to men a means of their salvation, is *a fortiori* excluded. That God hates lies, and that ethnic religions are lies, falsehoods, lying vanities, etc. is of course the constant language of Holy Scripture. On the other hand, promise-keeping is very often obviously not obligatory; but the circumstances that make it right or even obligatory for a man not to keep a promise arise from features of the human situation that cannot be transferred to God.

It is in fact easy to show that if God cannot lie, neither can he break his word. A man who is not lying when he makes a promise may nevertheless fail to fulfil it for a number of reasons. First, a man may simply change his mind for some reason or none, and decide not to keep his word. But God cannot change his mind capriciously, nor can new considerations occur to him. Secondly, a man may find the fulfilment of the promise impossible, owing to unforeseen circumstances or even owing to a hidden logical inconsistency in his plans. (A sufficiently absent-minded man may make some promises on the assumption that he has an appointment with a dentist and others on the assumption that this appointment has been cancelled; few of us are so absent-minded

as that, but a deeper-buried inconsistency in our plans may still elude us.) But God's plans can have no buried inconsistencies in them, nor can he ever be surprised by unforeseen circumstances. God can never be entrapped by his own promises as a man may be: God is like the Grand Master who makes a winning move, secure against all alternative lines of play his adversary may adopt. Thirdly, a man may decide that the performance of what he has promised would be wrong. The case where he decides this because of a change in circumstances is one to which there can be no parallel in God's case, for the reason already stated under the second head; and it is equally impossible that God should come to realize, as he previously did not, the wrongness of fulfilling some promise. So if God is altogether truthful, it is also absolutely excluded that he should fail to perform what he has sincerely promised. As the prophet says, it is not for our sakes, but for the sake of his Holy Name: it is not that by reneguing on his promises he would be inflicting injury or unkindness on us, but because he is Truth and cannot deny himself. Let us never despair if God's plain promises seem to be plainly unfulfilled and now unfulfillable; God will not fail or deny himself; he knows how to make straight our crooked ways that may seem to frustrate him.

I return to the question of the malice of lying. People speak sometimes as if this consisted in denying to others the truth which they have a right to be told. But this account is inadequate. Many rights can be defeated or forfeited: some hold this even for the right to live, and most people would hold it for many rights that are

clearly more important than a right to the truth can be. No need to imagine dramatic war-time circumstances: a declared private enemy of A in time of peace, whose enmity is of his own making, forfeits all sorts of claims he could have made on A if he had not broken with A; why not the right to truth from A? A good and sincere man cannot, I think, fail to hold that lying is evil; but may it not be a necessary evil in the circumstances, say as a weapon of self-defence?

One reason why lying might be defensible was already rejected in the last chapter, in my defence of legalism. We are simply not to consider whether in the circumstances a lie will produce the best possible consequences. We can neither foresee nor control the ultimate consequences of our actions: God can and does do both, and we cannot spoil his plan by not lying.

The trouble is that our judgment in this matter is liable to be corrupted by bad habits. We almost all have a habit of telling small gratuitous lies: of course many men are worse liars than this. But even this bad habit corrupts our practical wisdom. So in some crisis we find we can think of no alternative but to lie or to do something plainly much worse: and we lie. 'What else could I do?' The reply must be: 'Corrupted by your bad habits, you could do no better than you did. Do not therefore hold yourself guiltless. If you had been a better man, you would perhaps not have been in such a jam; or being in it, you could have extricated yourself without lying. You may say you lacked the wits to do this in the emergency: no doubt you did, but whose fault is that?'

It is because lying becomes second nature to us, so

much so that in a small way, or even in a big way, we
no longer know whether we are lying or not, that the
only counsel is total abstinence. It is not a matter of how
much we injure our neighbour by lying, as the 'right to
truth' theory maintains: it is a matter of how much we
damage our own souls, and make them inept for their
last end: to see and reflect the Living Truth. A moderate
drinker may never get drunk; a moderate liar who does
not lament and try to cure his ill habit will quite certainly one fine day come out with a big, whopping,
utterly inexcusable, lie. Total abstinence from lying is
what we should aim at; we may approach the goal before
we die.

It may be protested that without lying the work of the
world cannot be done. Some respected Christian figure,
I forget who, said that those who do the world's real
work cannot hope to keep their hands clean. No doubt:
but only to those who have clean hands and a pure heart,
who have not sworn deceitfully to their neighbour, is the
blessing of the LORD promised. Those who do the world's
work have their reward; the world passes away and the
plans and work of the world; but he who does the will
of God is God's own child, who can dwell in God's
house for ever.

If we read the lives of the Saints, we see how they
managed to avoid lying in crises. St Athanasius was
rowing on a river when the persecutors came rowing in
the opposite direction: 'Where is the traitor Athanasius?'
'Not far away,' the Saint gaily replied, and rowed past
them unsuspected. St Joan of Arc, I have read, used to
put a cross on her letters to her commanders to show that

114

the sentences bore the opposite of the normal French meaning. I suppose English intelligence failed to crack this code; anyhow, at her trial she was accused of lying, and of blasphemy to boot for using the cross. But surely she had a good defence; words get their meaning by convention, and her commanders, to whom the letters were addressed, knew the convention and were not misled; if English soldiers, who had no business to read her letters or to be in her country at all, read them and were misled, that was not her affair.

Such is the snakish cunning of the Saints, commended in the Gospel. When I used such examples in a paper many years ago, I was heard with some indignation: unsurprised, I heard mutterings about Jesuitry; though the Society of Jesus cannot be made responsible in any special way either for setting this sort of example or for the teaching that commends such equivocations. A Saint who by practice or precept shows us that we should not lie even in self-defence, but at most resort to equivocation, may be accused of Pharisaism and hypocrisy. I reply that the claim to be given scandal by this is itself hypocrisy like that of the Pharisees on the part of many. Your moral philosophers profess themselves literally *capable de tout*: you mention some frightful deed, and they at the drop of a hat will start constructing a case in which the deed would be *obligatory*; I have heard them at it. And these are the men who pretend to be shocked by the twisty mind of St Athanasius or St Joan! Kingsley expressed doubt and fear about whether Newman, committed as he was to the defence of this tradition about lying and equivocation, might not be

defensively using some cunning linguistic sleight; but at that rate how can I ever be sure that your moral philosophers have not some end in view which to their mind fully justifies them in lying to me? lying like troopers? Am I to trust Professors of Lying that they do not lie?

There is no doubt a persistent feeling that the out-and-out liar is a more straight-forward fellow – I remember from somewhere the French phrase *plus simple et plus loyal*, used in this connexion – than the man who will equivocate but not lie. Certainly a man who will very readily equivocate is likely to be a shifty character; it does not follow that we should say the same of a man who will in a suitable case equivocate, but simply will not lie. And if Christ really did speak of 'destroying this temple' when he meant his own Body, this was as far a stretch of equivocation as you will find defended in any example of St Alfonso de Liguori.

Some may say that to mislead others by equivocation, or even by silence, or by some action that gives a misleading impression – as when an escaping prisoner carries a plank like a workman – just *is* a lie. This is an evil hangover from the ways of bullying parents and guardians, well described in Kipling's story of his own childhood. *All* ways of escape and concealment must be closed: not only lying, to which a frightened child may resort, but other ways as well; and they must be *called* lying when they aren't, to give a suitable sense of guilt. Let us be men and put away these childish things. Silence really can be a lie, for in some circumstances it must mean assent, or must mean dissent, and the assent

or dissent would be a lie if spoken out loud; but it is a tricky business to specify such circumstances. The concept of acting a lie is of even more restricted legitimate application. Only an act that is a conventional sign of something can be a veracious or mendacious sign; an act that is not a conventional sign does not become an acted lie simply because it produces wrong impressions or disappointed expectations.

I turn now to the matter of making and breaking promises. It is a curiously common delusion of philosophers that promises, or at least the really important ones, are made by saying 'I promise', so that the peculiar force of these words is what we must above all investigate. Of course it is not so: nor can we shuck off the guilt of breaking our word as easily as the legendary Oxford moral philosopher, who thought that by saying 'I will' instead of 'I promise' he had reduced his obligation merely to that of sincerely expressing his intention at the moment. Marriage promises are no less binding if no words like 'I promise' or 'I plight my troth' are used in making them.

The mystery of 'I promise' is in its main lines easily cleared up: it is what may be called a logical back-formation. Philologists apply this term say to the verb 'to swashbuckle', which is formed as if 'swashbuckler' were its agent noun: in fact a swashbuckler is a man who swashes his buckler with his sword. I argue that 'I promise' is not related to 'he promises' as 'I breathe' is to 'he breathes', any more than 'swashbuckle' is related to 'swashbuckler' as 'bake' is to 'baker'. 'He promises' primarily relates to *certain* future-tense expressions of

intention; to express your intention to ϕ, in certain circumstances, is to promise to ϕ. But since normally 'I ψ', said of myself by myself, answers to 'He ψs', said by the other fellow of me, the form of words 'I promise to ϕ' has come into use as a substitute for the plain 'I will ϕ' in circumstances where that does constitute a promise; because these are circumstances in which the other fellow might say of me 'He promises to ϕ'. (One gets of course such half-way forms as 'I will ϕ; I promise that' or 'I will ϕ, and that's a promise.')

To see what constitutes promising, we need to consider what is added by the institution of promising over and above the sincere expression of intention. We can after all go a long way by relying on sincere expressions of intention. Railways do not contract to run trains at the times announced in the time-tables, and no action at law would lie against them for failing to do so; but if we believe in the veracity of the railway authorities, and find out by experience that they do not very readily depart from plans that they have formed and have truthfully announced, then we can successfully use railway time-tables for our future planning. But there are special reasons, which it would not be too hard to formulate, why the railways should form very stable plans.

In innumerable cases, however, the veracious announcement of an intention supplies no particular reason why a man should not later form a contrary intention. He may indeed have some obligation to announce his change of mind, if ignorance of this would inconvenience his neighbour; but he cannot be charged with lying, even if he did not announce his change of mind; nor has he

even concealed the truth to his neighbour's detriment, if he announced his change of mind as soon as it was definitive. Wherein then does the badness of promise-breaking lie? Though God's truthfulness excludes his breaking his word, a man can be quite truthful about his intentions and yet lay himself open to the reproach of promise-breaking. What is the force of the reproach?

We may gather an answer, I think, from the figure of speech 'You let us down.' The expression is a cliché, a dead metaphor: let us try to make the dry bones live. A announces his intentions; B, to A's knowledge, makes plans that will be frustrated, to B's great damage, if A changes his mind; even if A announces his change of mind. A's change of mind puts B in the sort of situation B would be in if he built on a foundation which he thought solid but which now crumbles beneath him: A has let B down. This is a paradigm case in which A may be charged not with mendacity, and perhaps not even with infirmity of purpose, but certainly with promise-breaking, even if A never said 'I promise' or 'I plight my troth' or the like words. And the injury that would be caused by letting somebody down is to my mind the source of the obligation that an expression of intention may give rise to, and is what makes the expression into a promise. At least this is very often the case: very often this is how the obligation of promise-keeping arises. I am of course here speaking only of one-sided promises; two-sided promises, promises exchanged between two parties, are covenants in Hobbes's sense, of which the lawyers' contracts are a special case; and these raise rather different problems.

If this is how the obligation of promisors arises, we see also how it may lapse or be overridden. If the promisee himself says 'I don't hold you to doing that', he is estopped from saying 'You let me down by not doing that': it is then no longer reasonable for him to expect performance from the promisor. Again, even if the promisee does not release him, the promisor is released from his obligation if the fulfilment of the promise will not benefit but injure the promisee: if the promisor now discovers this, or if circumstances change so that the promisee would now be injured by what previously would have benefited him. Finally, if the circumstances come to be such that A's fulfilment of his promise to B will injure C more than non-fulfilment will injure B, then whatever B may feel about the matter A is released, and it would be preposterous for B, knowing the circumstances, to reproach A for breaking his promise and letting B down.

The cases of promise-breaking in an emergency and lying in an emergency are to my mind quite different. It would be monstrous to ignore the wounded man by the wayside in order to keep a promise to buy something in a shop, whose lack would inconvenience your household; you should break your promise without hesitation and without shame. But if you tell a lie to avert some great evil, then you should be ashamed of yourself: you should have faith that the God whose Providence governs all things is a God of Truth who hates all lies, and at the same time is infinitely powerful and wise and does not require of any man a choice between sin and sin, though indeed the man himself by a previous sin may paint

himself into a corner. If you can *see* no way out but a lie, the lie may be the least wicked of the alternatives you can discern: it is still wicked, and you should blame yourself that you lacked the wisdom of St Joan or St Athanasius, to extricate yourself without lying. It is not a matter of foxy cleverness; 'the testimony of the LORD is sure and giveth wisdom to the simple'. And of course there are some lies that are absolutely excluded: lies that gravely injure your neighbour, including those that corrupt his understanding like the inculcation of false theory; or again perjuries, false swearings to which the God of Truth is made witness, or apostasy from the Faith. In such cases you are not to consider what evil may befall you, and yours, if you do not lie: you must tell truth and shame the Devil.

Vows, which are promises to God and one-sided at that, raise a special problem: God cannot be let down by expecting you to keep a vow that you break, nor can you anywise injure him,

> *semota a nostris rebus seiunctaque longe:*
> *nam privata dolore omni, privata periclis,*
> *ipsa suis pollens opibus, nil indiga nostri.*

Vows are not made for God's sake but for ours: our nature is weak, and a good resolution which it would be good to keep but not obligatory may easily wither away. If we bind ourselves so that it would be great and manifest sin to fail of performance, a vow may be justified: but in view of the risk of sin incurred by failure, men who are considering whether to strengthen their resolution by a vow should remember the parable

of the man who built only a folly because his funds for building a proper tower ran out.

Promises to the dead are another case moralists have considered. Injury to the dead is not out of the question: as Aristotle remarked in the *Ethics*, posthumous dishonour, or again injury to those a man has left behind him, is commonly accounted injury to a dead neighbour, or prospectively to oneself. And since the obligation of fulfilling a promise arises from the injury that would be done by non-fulfilment, there can be such obligations to the dead. But where the promisee cannot be injured by the non-fulfilment of the promise – certainly if he cannot be injured even notionally by the non-fulfilment, because being dead (or even merely absent) he will never know that a promise to him has been made of little account – then no obligation arises at all. A has privately promised, let us say, to some elderly friend B that A will not grow his hair long in the modern fashion that so much disgusts B; but B is dead, or away in Australia, and A's girl-friend likes long hair, and B will never know. I do not think A does B any wrong by letting his hair grow long. If B is dead or inaccessible, B cannot let A off his promise, and some philosophers are very solemn about promises to the dead on this account: but I say bluntly that to do something merely because you have promised a dead man – when you cannot do him even any posthumous injury – is at best irrational, and if it interferes with your neighbour's good is immoral.

I now come to covenants, promises exchanged. The obligation to keep covenant when the other party has kept his side, or when there is reasonable expectation that

he will, is a heavier obligation by far than the obligation to keep a one-sided promise. Without covenants' being made and generally observed, the amenities of civilized life would be largely made impossible. I think it is misconceived, for various reasons, to regard the authority of civil government as arising from some sort of covenant; but the need for civil authority arises, as Hobbes pointed out, because there is nothing easier to break than a man's word.

It is a calumnious misrepresentation of Hobbes to make him out as saying that the obligation of covenant arises only from there being a civil authority to enforce it: Hobbes was in fact rather rigorous in his doctrine of the obligations of covenant; he held that a prisoner of war was obliged to pay the ransom he had promised to pay in exchange for a promise of his life, and would apparently even hold that someone who promises a ransom to a criminal is obliged to pay it unless the civil law discharges him! To the protest that covenants made under fear are void, Hobbes sternly replies: 'that which could not hinder a man from promising ought not to be admitted as a hindrance of performing'. We need not, I think should not, go as far as that, but we may agree with Hobbes that covenants already, and of their nature, oblige: the civil authority, which enforces covenants, ties men being obliged, in Hobbes's phrase; and the need for covenants to be made, and then enforced against the perversity and lability of men's wills, is what brings the need of civil authority.

Civil authority is founded upon men's need of justice: Hobbes founds it on men's need of peace, but I think

this really comes to the same thing, given the way Hobbes spells out the notion of peace. And without justice civil authority is weakened in its claims upon us or lapses altogether. Professor Anscombe has put a dictum of Augustine's into English thus: Take away justice, and Government is just a big Syndicate; and she has illustrated the point by the story of the pirate who told Alexander the Great that the difference between them was only in the scale of their operations, and was rewarded with a satrapy for his wit. The mere fact that I enjoy the protection of a government gives me no obligation, no allegiance, to it if it is grossly unjust. If I had lived in the turbulent North at that time, I might have paid blackmail to Rob Roy or Johnny Armstrong in exchange for protection and lest a worse thing should befall me: that would nowise oblige me to protect Rob Roy or Johnny Armstrong from his fate if a stronger man than he should be likely to overcome him.

The character of many governments today is so grossly unjust (many of them are preparing to shed innocent blood in torrents, some are already shedding it) that I think a Christian justified in regarding them with as little favour as any blackmailing Border bandit of old or any protection racketeer in a big city of today; a citizen has not by accepting the protection covenanted his support, even if Hobbes supposed otherwise; and it is towering impudence for such creatures to conscribe men to fight for them. Bandits have done that too: we may remember the serving man in the ballad:

> Ye paid me well my hire, Lady,
> Ye paid me well my fee:

But noo I'm Edom o' Gordon's man –
Maun either do or dee.

I do not say that this gives a right of rebellion: the injustices of a Government may be substantial enough for A to think he has no allegiance to it without his thinking he has a right to bring upon the community the possibly extreme miseries of a rebellion. We should however remember that rebellions can be fairly bloodless: the 'Redeemer' Kwame Nkrumah was overthrown with the loss of life only of a few of his own hatchet-men, whom we need not worry about because, in Hamlet's words, they did make love to this employment.

What justice in civil society consists in has been admirably spelled out by Hobbes when he lists the laws of nature dictating peace for a means of the conservation of men in multitudes, and the various forms of vice opposed to the keeping of these laws:

1 Because men are unwilling to acknowledge natural inferiority, the law is not to recognise any such, even if there could be factual arguments for recognising it: Hobbes maintained this against Aristotle's claim that strong-bodied barbarian slaves were by nature mere tools of civilized men like himself, and we should maintain the like against such enemies of the human race as now urge discrimination against genetically inferior races of low average IQ.

Racialism is of course not the only form of that odious vice Pride: in past times there have been laws treating noblemen, men of quality, as if they were a superior kind of animal. Hume could still write 'The skin, pores, muscles, and nerves of a day-labourer are different from

those of a man of quality.' Hobbes had already answered this: 'as if Master and Servant were not introduced by consent of men but by difference of Wit; which is not only against reason but also against experience'. The profane habitually say (I read it recently in a school textbook of my daughter's) that the Law of Moses was not given by God but cribbed from the code of Hammurabi: they seem never to have noticed that the code of Hammurabi systematically discriminates between gentlemen and commoners, whereas the Divine Law lacks the very notion of a gentleman.

The inequality of slavery is an even grosser injustice: and on this matter there prevails gross ignorance of the wise, just, and merciful provisions of the Divine Law. Chattel slavery did not exist in Israel: the slave-dealer was liable to capital punishment. An Israelite could not kill his servant without paying life for life, and could not maim him by so much as knocking out a tooth without immediately losing his service. And a master could not break up a servant's family against his will. Moreover, any stranger who fled from slavery in a Gentile country was a free man the moment he stood on Israeli soil: we know that this law was enforced, because of the way Tacitus rails against it in his *Histories*. No wonder then that the profane textbook author I have cited depreciates the Jews, who superstitiously believed they had a Law given by God, in comparison with the Romans, who were continually improving their laws with the highest human wisdom!

2 No men are to claim for themselves, to the exclusion of others, such possessions as will impede the

others' 'right to govern their owne bodies; enjoy aire, water, motion, waies to go from place to place; and all things doe without which a man cannot live or not live well'. The denial of the right to speak one's native tongue is certainly to be counted as denial of that without which a man cannot live well. The vice that leads to breach of this law is Arrogance.

3   A judge between men is to deal equally between them; men who submit to an arbitrator voluntarily are to abide by his judgment; no man is to be judge in his own cause, or to arbitrate in a case in which 'greater profit, or honour, or pleasure apparently arises out of the victory of one party than of the other'. Judges are to give no arbitrary credit to one witness of fact rather than another. Breach of these laws tends to make men despair of any arbitrament except force and therefore manifestly militates against peace. The vices opposed to this are inequitableness ('Iniquity') and Acception of persons.

4   Men are to be grateful for benefits given them 'of mere grace'. The opposite vice is Ingratitude. The accusation of ingratitude is likely to be made by unjust rulers and their toadies and court-chaplains against their non-cooperative subjects; this, as I have said, is mere impudence.

5   Men are to strive to accommodate themselves to others and in particular to abstain from open expression of hatred and contempt.

6   A man has to pardon offences of the penitent if he has security for their future good conduct and is not to repay evil for evil out of mere revenge; punishment by the civil authority should have regard to correction of

the offender or the instruction and deterrence of others, not to vengeance for past sins. It is manifest that the vice of cruelty in retaliation is hostile to peace; and how dare we indulge our vengeance when we are all sinners? I have read that in old Spain the King on Good Friday would release a condemned criminal, kiss his hand, and ask for his prayers. No doubt such a ceremony is inconceivable in our society: I remember how a proposal for an amnesty for army deserters many years after the War on some joyful national occasion was shouted down with a cry of 'Not fair!' – a cry that is all too often just a yelp of envy, hatred, and malice.

These principles, set forth in *Leviathan*, c.15, are not exhaustive of natural justice: there is for example the principle that only a man, not his kindred, is to be punished for offences; a principle insisted upon by Hobbes, as it is in the Divine Law and the Prophets, and of course flagrantly flouted in the Roman Law. I have not space here to develop these matters at length.

University people argue mightily about whether laws that violate these principles are laws or (as Aquinas called them) mere violence. Of course it doesn't matter whether you *call* them laws or not: the question is what consequences follow. An unjust piece of legislation exists *de facto*, as an institution: but it is no debt of justice to observe it, though it may be imprudent to ignore it. And though a private person should not lightly judge a law to be unjust, its contrariety to the Law of Nature and the peace and justice of society may be so manifest that such judgment is assured. A sufficient mass of unjust legislation may justify a man in deciding that the civil authority

is a mere Syndicate; I think Old John Brown rightly so judged about the slave-owning US commonwealths of his time. Rebellion, however, is another matter, because the evils it may bring are so great: whether Old John Brown judged rightly about this is a matter we must leave between Old John Brown and his Maker, to whose judgment he so confidently appealed.

The laws of man, Heraclitus said, are all fed by the one Divine Law: God's justice also gives human laws their force, and God is just not only as true and faithful, but as the giver of the Divine Law, both naturally to men's minds and externally by Revelation. God cannot be grateful to men or enter into a contract for mutual benefit as man can with man: God owns already, *de jure* and *de facto*, all that man might give him; except that God leaves to man the choice of obedience and disobedience; and that is why obedience is better than sacrifice.

> Our wills are ours, we know not how:
> Our wills are ours, to make them Thine.

I have said little in this chapter of the now much agitated topic of justice as fair distribution. I find the topic too difficult to discuss in this work if it regards justice as between men; but it is quite clear that God has no regard at all for justice as fairness, either here or hereafter. In this life, and as regards what medievals called the goods of fortune, God gives men only the fairness of a fair lottery; he is, as Thackeray called him, the Ordainer of the lottery. Such things as outbreaks of war and peace, deaths in epidemics, and deaths by

various sorts of accidents are distributed by the rules of a lottery: by promulgating to our minds the rational standards of probability judgment, and showing us in our lives that these standards are observed, God plays fair with us. As was said of M. Blanc of Monte Carlo, red wins sometimes and black wins sometimes, but White always wins. But these goods of fortune are clearly distributed neither equally nor with any regard to merit. The Book of Job and the words of Jesus Christ contain emphatic repudiations of the idea that good and evil fortune in this life go by merit; and experience continually shows how true are the words of the Preacher: 'I saw that under the Sun the race is not to the swift, nor the battle to the strong, nor riches to the learned, nor favour to the skilful, but time and chance in all.'

As for the enduring and genuine goods, grace and glory, there is no reason to believe that God observes any principle of justice as fairness; no reason to believe that all men get an equal share, or even an equal chance of an equal share, of grace and glory. All that we can say is that each man gets a genuine chance of salvation, and it is his own fault if he rejects it; but that God should give A no further chance and repeat his invitation to B is indeed mercy to B, but not unfairness to A. And if C, who like B is saved, has laboured longer and harder than B, he has no grudge against B for winning salvation on easier terms. 'Take what is thine and go thy way; I will also give to the last even as to thee.'

7

TEMPERANCE

Justice is, or ought to be, an exciting topic: temperance is not. If I had wished to draw an enlarged audience, I might have announced a chapter on 'Gluttony, Drink, Drugs, and Sex', without meretricious misrepresentation of my range of topics; and such a title might have been mildly exciting. But the virtue of temperance is a humdrum, common-sense matter. Unlike prudence and justice, temperance is not an attribute of God; it cannot even be ascribed to the holy angels, for it can belong only to animals with bodily needs and appetites. And men need temperance because they need to observe a mean of virtue if they are to pursue and attain any great or worthy end: if they are neither to be distracted from the end by the pursuit of short-term enjoyments, nor to damage their bodily and mental health by excessive abstinence. These considerations are not such as to arouse enthusiasm: indeed, someone who was enthusiastic about temperance would be in danger of falling into the vice, for which we have no special name, that is the opposite extreme to intemperance. I do not wish to deny that the virtue of chastity, and its highest form the virtue of virginity, can be passionately loved, defended, and admired; but I shall argue that it is a Hellenizing distortion to bring these under the heading of temperance.

Aristotle remarks in regard to temperance that the

131

mean between excess and defect set by this virtue is relative to the case: a reasonable diet for a man doing severe exercises for the Olympic Games might be grossly excessive for an ordinary citizen. It is to this principle that we must appeal if the extreme ascetic practices of some Christian Saints are not to be regarded as vicious practices, opposed to the virtue of temperance by excess as intemperate self-indulgence is by defect. Whether the practices are justified depends on the truth or falsehood of dogmas for which I cannot here argue: the dogma of the Communion of Saints, whereby the good deeds of one member of Christ's Body can redound to the benefit of other members; and again, the doctrine that the great Saints are like God's élite Brigade of Guards against our invisible enemies, who are ingenious, ruthless, and untiring; and that therefore the Saints' watching and praying and fasting and severe discipline is needful to preserve the city from the enemy.

Asceticism is often admired by Christians on these grounds, and I think rightly: but of course it does not follow that the greater the asceticism, the more it should be admired. There are certain clear limits that asceticism must not transgress, and if it does so the transgression is fatal to any claim of sanctity. The mutilation or immobilization of a limb, self-castration, deprivation of one of the special senses, reduction of the intellect to imbecility by depriving it of its proper nourishment of thought: all this is manifest sin and vice. Happily such vice is rare in the West, just as it was in Aristotle's Greece; but it is to be found sometimes as a manifestation of a morbid self-hatred. Elsewhere under

the aegis of false religion the vice flourishes, in forms too repellent to describe. A Hindu is reported to have said to a Christian missionary, with manifest truth, that their yogins practised far more extreme asceticism than Christian Saints; the missionary of course ought not to have felt any shame or embarassment on hearing this; the Saints had not put themselves down, after all, for this particular competition.

I turn to the vices of gluttony and drunkenness. As regards gluttony there is a Latin line enumerating five varieties of gluttony by means of five adverbs: *praepropere, nimis, ardenter, laute, studiose*. Eating your food too quickly (*praepropere*), in excess (*nimis*), or too eagerly (*ardenter*), is prejudicial to health, and may be gravely so; eating too expensively (*laute*) or making a fuss about having everything you eat just right (feeding *studiose*) may lead to a seriously vicious way of living, with neglect of justice (like the rich man in the parable who let Lazarus rot outside his house) or of charity (as in the study of a selfish old woman that we find in Lewis's *Screwtape Letters*). Too much attention of any sort to the belly diverts the vital energies from what is worthier and provides ammunition for the enemy's attacks on chastity. It is manifest however that a man may be noticeably rather gluttonous without being grievously vicious.

Alcohol always takes the fine edge off intellectual performance, even in small doses, and impairs the efficient execution of skilled tasks. If it were a duty to be mentally as much alert as possible for as long as possible, this might speak against any consumption of

alcohol at all. But of course there is no such duty; we saw before, when we were discussing the greatest happiness of the greatest number, that such double comparatives or superlatives as we get in 'being as mentally alert as possible for as long as possible' raise logical difficulties. Aquinas has remarked that it is a precept of reason that the exercise of reason should be intermitted; in sleep, and again in the sex act, this is quite normally the case; and again, there is nothing immoral in taking sleeping-pills or having a doctor give you anaesthetics for an operation.

If drinking alcohol is wrong, the reason is not that it makes you less alert than you might possibly be, but that it makes you less alert than you then and there ought to be; and the degree to which you ought to be alert varies very much. An extreme degree of alertness is rightly to be demanded of a railway signalman or of a car driver in heavy traffic. On the other hand, while I cannot answer for the efficacy as a cure for colds or influenza of hot toddy self-administered in bed till you pass out unconscious, if the medical theory is right the moral objection to drunkenness vanishes; a man safe tucked up in bed has no duty for even the lowest degree of alertness, for he could lawfully just go to sleep. There are many intermediate cases, into the casuistry of which I will not enter.

If we may for the moment abstract from the question whether the law-breaking that may be involved is morally objectionable, then we ought, I think, to judge about *cannabis indica* much as we judge about alcohol; and *cannabis indica* appears to be less mentally disturbing than alcohol, less productive of damaging accidents

like car crashes, and very much less addictive. The allegation that use of it 'leads on' to the use of dangerous drugs like cocain and heroin is complete nonsense; smoking cannabis does not create any physiological need for these drugs, nor can it lead on to the use of these drugs unless they are there to be used.

So far I have only considered the relaxation of the intellect from the height of attentiveness; a height, let me repeat, that we have no obligation to try to maintain. It is another matter when we consider 'blowing your mind': that is, deliberately seeking what can only be called a state of temporary insanity. What are called psychedelic drugs are only one way to this state; ether vapour and nitrous oxide were more old-fashioned ways (as is recorded in William James), and yet other ways are peculiar breathing exercises, and again that repetition of some meaningless utterance, *battologia*, which was and is characteristic of Gentile religion, and as such was condemned in the Sermon on the Mount. Whatever way the thing is done, it appears to me a detestable abuse of the faculty that distinguishes us from the brute; I shall not argue the matter, for a man who requires argument to persuade him that sanity is preferable to insanity is already in such a sad state that argument is unlikely to do him any good.

In defence of such practices it is often said that they distract only the sensory and imaginative powers; the intellect is left to observe and describe what happens. But I can see no evidence for this claim and much against it. Professor R. C. Zaehner recorded that under a psychedelic drug he saw one of the Three Kings in an

135

icon trying to pull off his crown, which being only two-dimensional he was unable to do; this made Zaehner giggle, and he went on giggling till the drug wore off. Now this story has on the face of it only the limited coherence of a dream-report; and if Zaehner had said he dreamt this rather than that he saw it by aid of a drug, no claim would be made about the remarkable clarity of the observing intellect that is required in order to make such a report. Zaehner, indeed, does not make any such claim; he is as sceptical as I am about the benefits of blowing your mind.

Other reports make a good deal less sense than Zaehner's. If a man reports that for him under his drug the hedge in the garden is the Dharma body of Buddha, I am not immediately convinced that he knows what he is talking about. And I remember a University colleague, many years ago, asking me what I thought of the report that a drug had been known to disturb a subject's private time-flow, so that the subject encountered numerically the same events several times over. He was very solemn about it, and regarded me, no doubt, as a dreadful Philistine when I replied 'All it shows me is that if you hop up your brain with a drug you start talking nonsense.'

From the outside some of the experiences of Old Testament prophets are certainly hard to distinguish from mere insanity; somebody who today acted like the prophet Ezekiel would soon be locked up. But there is one marked difference between Ezekiel and the mind-blowers; his experience did not come because he *sought* a vision by spiritual or physical exercises or by drug-

taking; they came unasked, even unwelcome. It is no doubt only an accident of the word-choice made by English translators, but it is very suitable that a prophet's visions should be called the *burden* of the Lord.

I turn then to the topic of chastity. Hellenic thought regarded the sexual appetite as simply one of the bodily appetites governed by the virtue of temperance; and Aquinas tried accordingly to fit in the virtue of chastity under the heading of temperance. He tried, but it was pretty clear in advance that he could not succeed; the shoe will not fit the foot. The sexual appetite is for one thing unique among bodily appetites in its likelihood to produce new individuals; creatures of another race might find themselves liable to bud off new individuals if they overate, but we are in no such danger. And likewise on account of this causal fact we can forget about the sexual mores of cultures where the facts about paternity are otherwise regarded; people who regard the ways of such a tribe as relevant to our enquiries are misguided.

We simply know that sexual intercourse is liable to lead to childbearing; and we can no more sensibly deliberate in abstraction from such knowledge, or give parity of esteem to the mores of those who lack it, than we could sensibly abstract from our knowledge that certain substances are needed for health and certain others are toxic. There are those who would say we cannot judge and condemn a culture from outside like this; be it so; the conception of paternity we have is part of our culture; here we are, and we can only work out our morals using this concept; the morals of people with a divergent concept are irrelevant to us. I am not saying

that this physiological fact of itself dictates our moral code; but it is still being appealed to in a moral code which allows for the avoidance or prevention of impregnation by one means or another.

Another big difference between chastity and temperance is concerned with what moral theologians call parvity of matter. A mild degree of gluttony or alcoholic intoxication is a very trifling offence; even a settled habit of such offences may deserve to be called only a fault, not a vice. In regard to unchastity, Christian moral theology holds it is much easier to sin grievously in the individual act, and there can be no question but that a bad habit is a vice. This stern view clearly appears to go back to the Founder's charter; let us remember his words about lecherous looks at a woman, and his promulgation of a precept about marriage which appeared to the Apostles so rigorous that they protested 'In that case it's better not to get married at all!'

These differences have been explained in some Christian apologetics by an argument that the sexual appetite can be lawfully indulged only in ways conformable to the built-in teleology of the generative organs in their structure and function. Other use of the generative organs has been compared to the use of the digestive organs by a Roman glutton who ate intending to vomit and then eat again. I myself once followed this line of thought, but it now appears to me radically defective. The appeal to teleology strikes me as fallacious; and anyhow the argument fails of its purpose, to afford a rationale for traditional Christian sexual morality.

The latter failure is quite easily demonstrated. It is a

use of the generative organs in a way irrelevant to any generative teleology to copulate with a woman who is pregnant, known to be barren, or past the menopause; but Christian tradition has not condemned such intercourse – for the last practice of course there are Scriptural precedents of holy married couples to cite, like Abraham and Sarah or the parents of St John the Baptist. Nor is it at all common for Christians to consider as morally binding upon them the prohibition in the Mosaic Law against copulation during the menstrual period. This precept quite clearly tends to exclude infertile intercourse, but Christians have not on that account accepted it; they have on the contrary regarded the Mosaic precept as one of the laws of ritual uncleanness that Christians simply don't need to bother about. The objection to intercourse at such a time would be on hygienic or aesthetic grounds, not on the score that the generative teleology of the act is being frustrated.

The argument about the teleology of the generative process seems to me to be vitiated by a simple underlying fallacy: the semantic confusion about the word 'end', which in English, as in Greek and Latin, can mean *both* the last stage of a process *and* the point of the process, what it is for. (Some languages are better off in this matter: German can distinguish unequivocally between *Ende* and *Zweck*, and Polish correspondingly between *koniec* and *cel*.) The generative process of living things is a cycle, in which no stage can readily be picked out as giving the whole process its point. Consider the life-cycle of the mayfly. The adult mayfly lives only for a day; it lacks digestive organs, I believe it lacks even mouth-

parts, and it merely has enough stored energy to succeed in mating and continuing the race. Are we to say that the end of the process is that this manifestly imperfect adult form should be generated by the transformation of the grub; or rather, that the male and female mayfly should have their one crowded hour of glorious life?

Aristotle was not himself always captivated by the misleading word *telos;* he could not be, for he held that the unceasing movement of the everlasting spheres which attain no final optimum position, is yet not devoid of point. He would say that both these cycles and the sublunary cycle of generation had as their point to manifest after their kind the everlasting life of God; and a Christian can go further, and see here a reflection of the eternal Divine generation, a thought expressed in the lines of Yeats:

> Natural and supernatural with the selfsame ring are wed
> As man, as beast, as an ephemeral fly begets,
> Godhead begets Godhead;
> For things below are copies, the Great Smaragdine
> Tablet said.

Now the argument I am opposing holds on the contrary that the production of the adult form can simply be read off from the generative process as its manifest end. I have given reason to reject this view; and though I have argued that conduct which runs athwart our built-in teleologies in a radical way, like conscientious objection to our dependence on consuming other life, is doomed to ruinous failure, this clearly does not mean that we should pursue as conscious goals all and only those goals which we can discern as written into the

teleologies of our organism. So the line of argument I am discussing now appears to me irremediably faulty.

All the same, there is a continuous tradition in the Christian Church of teaching that many forms of sexual behaviour that the pagans accepted ought to be regarded as manifest sin and vice. The past existence of this tradition comes out, for example, in Noonan's study *Contraception*, hostile as Noonan is to the present maintenance of the tradition. And in spite of the logical badness, to my mind, of the arguments I have just given in favour of the tradition, I accept the content of the tradition as sound and I shall myself try to defend it.

It is a general and indisputable logical point that refutation of a bad argument for a conclusion has not even a tendency to show the conclusion is false. Nevertheless, when I hang on to the traditional Christian view about sexual vices but now reject the line of argument by which I would formerly have defended the view, this may strike people as highly irrational. Some comparisons will, I hope, show that the attitude need not be irrational. An elder sister left in charge of her little brother may have to enforce certain restrictions on his behaviour; her parents have told her that certain things are forbidden; and the parents, let us suppose, had good reason for their prohibitions. If the young brother now says 'Why shouldn't I?' and argues the matter, the sister's attempt to find a rationale for the prohibitions may be a failure, and the young brother may be sharp enough to detect this; but he would be a young fool if on this account he decided to ignore the prohibitions. To use another comparison, there is the familiar story of the wise old Judge

telling his younger colleague to begin by not giving legal reasons for judicial decisions; the reason for this was that he thought the younger man had enough knowledge of and feeling for the law to be mostly right in his decisions, but was likely to muddle things if he tried to spell out the reasons for his decisions.

Similarly, I should argue, Christians have much more reason to expect the guidance of the Holy Ghost in the Church's substantive moral teaching than in the supplying of arguments to support this teaching. The aim here, to quote Aristotle, is not understanding but action; what most matters is that men should do the right things and do them in the right attitude of will, not that they should have a well-worked-out rationale of why these are the right things to do. If the Christian religion is true at all, if the promises of Christ are worth anything, then we may be confident that a moral teaching in the Church with a clear tradition and firm in its main outline is no deception; that apologetic attempts to justify the teaching should be infected with human errors is only to be expected and ought not to give scandal.

Let me turn to another element of Christian moral teaching; the prohibition of suicide. Here, as over sexual morality, there was a sharp conflict between the Church's teaching and the ethos of the pagan milieu in which the Church first developed; and the tradition against suicide is old, clear, and sharply defined. I shall argue presently that the connexion between the two topics, sex and suicide, is closer than might at once appear; and I think it is no accident that in our time the rebellions against the Church's tradition on these two topics are taking place

simultaneously and with a considerable overlap of the persons concerned; humanist enemies of Christianity and false brethren among Christians are very often found to advocate both euthanasia (that is, suicide to escape pain and disability) and a 'rethought' sexual morality.

Now the arguments against suicide are often as bad as the arguments in defence of traditional Christian sexual morality. The argument that suicide is self-murder is none the better for its antiquity. As Antony Flew once pointed out, you might equally condemn matrimonial intercourse, as own-wife adultery; both as regards 'x kills y' and as regards 'x copulates with y's wife', identifying the variables so that you have 'x' both times makes a difference that may well be morally relevant. Again, the argument that suicide cuts off a chance to repent of what you have done may suffice to show that *if* suicide is a sin it is a very great sin, but cannot be used to show that suicide *is* a sin.

All the same, I do not doubt that suicide is very wicked indeed. My solid ground for saying this is that I rely on Christian tradition in the matter; my argument in defence of the tradition is my own, and I hope that if it were shot down I'd still take the same view about suicide. It is an argument that ties in with what I said before. Our morality has to fit in with what we are and where we are, with our actual nature and position in the order of things: otherwise it is just irrelevant. And along with the idea of a do-it-yourself kit for devising moral codes I reject the idea that what we have to do is to intuit relations of fittingness that hold by some conceptual necessity between our actions and their circumstances.

Temperance

This is a British moral-philosophy tradition, exemplified quite recently in some of C. D. Broad's writings; we may well suspect it underlies the use in ethical argument of some of the fantastic biological suppositions I have come across; we are asked to suppose a woman giving birth to a normal healthy puppy, or a drug that could make kittens grow into rational animals, or people-seed that drifts in the air and may take root in your Aubusson carpet. The only theory on which such suppositions deserve to be taken seriously, and not just curtly dismissed with the Tommy Traddles response 'It isn't so, you know, so if you please we won't suppose it' – at least the only rationale I can make out – is the theory that in ethics we are meant to be trying to discern *a priori* relations of fittingness, to which it would be irrelevant whether those characteristics of actions or circumstances on which the fittingness is founded are ever physically exemplifiable. I see no reason to trust our competence to draw up moral programmes for such possible worlds; I shall stick to our world.

Now I hold that Original Sin is a grim pervasive fact about the human condition; and it is possible to think this even if you do not share Christian faith and hope about the remedy for this condition; possible, because this actually has been thought by great non-Christian thinkers, notably Schopenhauer. And Schopenhauer thought that suicide, so far from being any remedy or evasion of that misdirected will which is our bane, is the final desperate self-assertion of the evil will. For Schopenhauer, the pain or misfortune that is a temptation to suicide is like the touch of the surgeon's knife that could cut away at its

roots the diseased tissue; *finditur nodus cordis*. But the man of obstinate bad will who then commits suicide is like the cowardly patient who keeps his disease rather than face the painful operation. Consider a pure case: some evil ruler or big swindler who has no earthly chance of escape except by suicide; it is clear that in him the voluntarily sought death is no renunciation of the evil will, quite the contrary.

The opposite side of the same coin is presented in R. L. Stevenson's short story *Markheim*. Young Markheim, having just murdered a man in order to rob his antique shop, finds himself confronted by the Devil, in human shape, who hails him as an old acquaintance, and proceeds to show how hopelessly Markheim is in his toils; let him not think of cashing in on this crime and leading a better life on the proceeds. Their discussion is interrupted by the maid-servant's ringing the street door-bell. The Devil quickly urges Markheim to lure her in and murder her, so that he has all night to ransack the house at leisure. But Markheim has had enough. Convinced by the Devil that his life must be unfruitful of good, he resolves that it shall at least bear no more evil. With the feeling of a sailor who has reached port after a stormy voyage, he lets in the maid and tells her to fetch the police. And at that very moment – as if Stevenson wished to present visually what Schopenhauer meant by the conversion of the will – the sardonic features of the Devil change to the features of an angel, and even as they change dissolve and disappear.

All this is no digression: fixing our attention on Original Sin is the best way to begin the consideration of

sexual morality. The sexual desire which we share with the animals is of course not itself Original Sin, and the Genesis story should not be taken to mean that the first sin was a sexual one. All the same, there is clearly an intimate connexion between human sexuality as it now is (we need not speculate about sex acts in Paradise before the Fall) and Original Sin; for it is normally by sex acts that Original Sin in transmitted to a new generation; though I argued that it is equally transmitted by artificial insemination, and would be transmitted if other such devices, say artificial parthenogenesis, became possible. I shall try to spell out as carefully as I can what I take the relation to be.

In the corruption of Original Sin, in the misdirection of human teleologies, the whole man is involved; there is not a plurality of souls, or something like that, so that one part could be infected and not another. And man's generative powers and appetites are of necessity specially corrupted; for they are the very means by which the aboriginal corrupt appetite perpetuates itself. It follows that in the present state of things a plunge into sex is of its nature a plunge into the strong current running the wrong way – running too fast for us to swim against it – *unless* some special Divine aid is provided.

Christians hold that for this enormous evil God provided a remedy at once, not waiting till the Incarnation: the great good of marriage. Despite all human wickedness and all deformation of the marital institution, the greatness of this good is very visible, even apart from Christian or Jewish tradition. 'Nothing finer and nobler,' says Ulysses in the Odyssey, 'than for two of one mind

to dwell together in a house', for the sake of that great good, Penelope lay alone in faithful love for many years, and Ulysses preferred going home to his ageing wife above embraces of a goddess with youth and immortality thrown into the bargain, 'for he thought,' says Aristotle, commenting on the story, 'that immortality won by vice was the greatest of evils'. So also it was in the old Roman idea of a *confarreatio*, breaking bread together, that should bind two together for life.

Faithful marriage, union of flesh and heart and mind, is capable of neutralizing the corruption of sex in fallen man, so far as the spouses themselves are concerned. Complete healing there cannot be in this world; for the offspring of the best marriage will be born in Original Sin, to live perilously as their parents did; but for all that children are the blessing and the crown of marriage, for with the re-embodiment and reindividuation of the unhappily corrupt radical ancestral appetite there comes a new intellect, and with it a chance that in this individual the new will should be enlightened and directed aright; for all men there is grace offered, and the hope of glory.

Apart from the good of marriage that redeems it, sex is poison. It is not a matter of lower animal appetites, shared with ancestral apes, that overcome a weak will; the radical perversion or misdirection of the will is what deforms animal appetite. So it is that man has become so strongly lecherous, to a degree quite unknown among the apes; no use blaming them! A priest who had become a court-chaplain of the wicked world wrote a pamphlet that admitted man's great lechery; the Fathers would have seen here the plainest evidence of Original Sin; but this

fellow saw rather an enrichment of our life, worthy of the dignity of a rational creature!

So it is, likewise, that men are so variously and exquisitely lecherous: they must have their 57 varieties; and here again deliberate perversion far outdoes any animal abnormalities. There is a fashion for males to submit to surgical mutilation, like Nero's favourite Sporus, in order to play the female role; I even read a story written by the parents of a young girl whose psychiatrist advised her that her psyche was male, and who underwent a grim series of medical and surgical treatments to make her body conform to this alleged maleness; with an end result that must on any view have been unsatisfactory. But I have no desire to emulate St Peter Damian and gave you a Book of Gomorrah.

Nothing could be more false than the intended sense of the slogan 'Make love, not war'. Man's extreme and ingenious murderousness and his extreme and varied lechery are two aspects of his corruption; and neither, on the available evidence, can be blamed on apish ancestors, for the anthropoids are very much less lecherous than men and also much less disposed than men to kill within their own species: they wholly lack the practice of war. Cruelty is not the result of a buried lechery denied expression: in corrupt societies extreme degrees of cruelty and lechery have often coexisted. Schopenhauer rightly saw a symbol of this in Shiva, the god of destruction and murder who is also the god of the lingam or phallus; and so too Heraclitus said that Dionysus in whose honour men sing the phallic song is none other than Hades. And in false religions indeed the same deity is

often honoured by lechery and cruelty simultaneously; as in Mexico by ritual sodomy and enormous human sacrifices.

Let us turn from there to better themes; breathe the air of mountain heights rather than fetid streets. Marriage is a great good but not the best: virginity, a total consecration to the love of God that excludes human sexual love, is the best, the most glorious victory over our corruption. Schopenhauer saw this, and could not but see as a most appropriate symbol of the victory that overcomes the world the redemption of mankind by a virginal male born of a virgin mother. For him, as I said, this was only a myth; we cannot he held, conceptualize the goal of the converted will. For Christians it is no myth; but Schopenhauer, on the outside looking in, beheld in the faces of the Saints that peace for which he vainly longed. Schopenhauer was far, I fear, from the Kingdom of God, but not so far as those claiming the Christian name who hate the very idea of the Virgin Mother.

The high ideal of virginal dedication is not for all; but none of us can tell what may be demanded of us. God has not engaged himself not to demand great things of any one of us; anybody may be called on to live out bravely a virginal life, like Penelope waiting for Ulysses. So nobody can safely settle for a mediocre degree of virtue: 'Be perfect, as your Father in Heaven is perfect.'

8

COURAGE

It is appropriate that the virtue dealt with in the last chapter of this book should be courage. For courage is the virtue of the end: what makes a man endure to the end and in the extremity of evil. Courage is what we all need in the end; we all have to die, and for none of us can the possibility be excluded of dying nastily: in great pain, or after a long disabling illness.

Courage is constantly needed in the ordinary course of the world; in the *Screwtape Letters* the evil spirit laments that he and his fellows can only win very temporary success in getting men to depreciate courage, for God their enemy has so made the world that its afflictions and dangers show up the necessity and loveliness of courage. All the same, in academic circles in England such depreciation appears to be something of an intellectual fashion. I remarked in the first chapter of this book upon Hare's very curious deliberate assimilation of 'Courage is obviously admirable' to 'Niggers are obviously despicable' (see his *Freedom and Reason* pp. 187–9), and his depreciation of 'so-called "physical" courage' (p. 149). He holds that it would be hazardous to maintain that physical courage is 'upon the whole conducive to human well-being', at any rate in modern society. I read a draft of that chapter at a number of

English universities, and was not particularly surprised to find there more sympathy with Hare's attitude than with mine.

To defend courage is to labour the obvious; but we who defend it have no need to fear the charge that we are appealing to the meaning of words or making what we say true by definition. Courage is needed because of hard facts about the way the world will always be till Judgment Day. To say a truth is uncontestable is not to make it true in virtue of the meaning of words: as Norman Malcolm has remarked, 'There are a lot of dogs around' and 'Many men wear shoes' are both uncontestably true, even though so far as the meaning of words goes dogs might be as extinct as dodos and shoes as obsolete as togas.

Let us then attend to those plain facts about how men live and must live which make courage necessary. For a start, as Chesterton remarked, people would often not be born but for the courage of their mothers; this truth is more obvious nowadays when motherhood is more a matter of choice. A well-conducted early abortion is physically much safer than pregnancy endured to full term; at least, so the abortionist lobby would have it, and I do not wish to contest their statistics; and contraception is undoubtedly safer still. Even apart from the risk that childbearing will result in death or in permanent physical impairment, carrying a baby to full term may call for considerable endurance. If it came about that in very large proportion women were no longer willing to endure pregnancy and risk their lives in childbirth, then the human race would end; high time too, if it

had become so corrupt. But we have God's promise that till Kingdom Come seedtime and harvest shall not fail, and we can trust that till then the blessing of children will not fail either.

Again, our bodies are highly vulnerable, constantly exposed to peril of injury and death; but if we were always worrying about how to protect them, we should be cut off from very many activities, lose much enjoyment, suffer many inconveniences, and be continually plagued by painful apprehension. Nobody who was thoroughly cowardly would play physically demanding games, or climb a mountain, or ride a horse or a bicycle. Hare himself writes: 'Perhaps, however, men ought to reconcile themselves to being complete cowards unless they are convinced that they can do nothing about it.' (*Freedom and Reason*, p. 155) Indeed not: a modicum of courage is needed by the least athletic of us if he is to live in a modern city. If a man's foolish parents have let him grow up a thorough coward, it may indeed be difficult for him to do anything about it; good reason why parents should avoid this folly.

It is mere thoughtlessness on Hare's part to say that in modern society courage is a 'human excellence whose utilitarian basis is vestigial' (p. 149). The Russians speak of Heroes of Labour, and it is no empty word. Without a great deal of patient endurance and of courage in emergencies coal would not be mined nor steel forged nor the seas fished; our society rests on the shoulders of these brave men, who like Housman's army of mercenaries 'save the sum of things for pay'. Not long ago a young lorry driver gave his life to steer his vehicle out

of harm's way when the brakes failed; he died as gallantly as any soldier.

Clearly Hare forgets this everyday civilian courage when he suggests that courage is no longer needed 'in the present state of military science' (a thesis that I do not think the Israelis or the Egyptians would accept); like Plato and Aristotle, he makes courage in battle the paradigm. It was natural for Greek philosophers to do this, given the continual wars of the Greek city-states; and in reading them we can and should enter into their situation with imaginative sympathy; but that does not mean we need think of courage primarily in military terms.

The ordinary course of the world, even in times of peace, is so ordered that men regularly need some courage, and some men sometimes need very great courage; courage to endure, courage to face the worst. And few people are really likely to be persuaded that courage is not certainly admirable: but there is more likelihood that people should come to regard courage as an ideal to be admired, rather than an everyday virtue that is to be expected of us. The Roman Church applies the term 'heroic virtue' to canonized Saints; the term has come into common use to mean a virtue that is rarely found in men and women of heroic mould but is not to be expected of ordinary folk. This is a cunning snare of Hell's Philological Arm. An emergency offering only the alternatives of being very brave and being guilty, by act or omission, of something very shameful is something that nobody can be sure will not come his way in the course of life. Or again, a man may have to endure for a long time some affliction from which there is only a shameful

escape. All is not lost for a man who fails under such a test if he acknowledges his guilt; then there is a chance of contrition and amendment; but it is absolute death to the soul if he comforts himself with the thought 'It would have been heroic virtue; and I'm no hero – it was not to be expected of me.'

A man has no right to demand that he shall never be put in circumstances that call for courage and endurance: no claim of this sort can be made upon his fellow-men; still less upon God. To the plea 'I'm no hero' the reply may be made: 'You are a hero, in the Greek sense of the word: a son not just of mortal parents, but of God.' As I said before, when out of a zygote endowed with merely vegetative life there comes to be a rational creature endowed with discourse of reason and free choice, this is a daily miracle: something that in principle cannot be explained in the categories that suffice to describe sub-rational nature, but only by special Divine intervention; this is the Finger of God. The King stamps his image on each coin, and then the mould is broken, so that no coin just like this one is ever struck again. Anybody who imaginatively grasps the wonder of this will not feel disposed to think that 'science makes it impossible for thoughtful people to accept the Virgin Birth'; what these thoughtful people call 'science' cannot explain the birth of any man, let alone that Man.

Believing that they are sons of God, how should men live? Alexander the Great, it appears, really believed his wicked mother's story that he was the son not of his mortal putative father Philip, but of Zeus. The belief perhaps lasted all his life. But Alexander's reaction (no

doubt it helped him that he was Aristotle's pupil) was to decide that he must live worthily of his divine origin. He must love wisdom and virtue, rule justly, be foremost in courage and endurance when waging war, and show mercy and generosity to his enemies in the hour of victory. Such was Alexander's ideal; he strove to live up to it, and was bitterly repentant when he failed (as in the drunken manslaughter of his friend Kleitos).

What then of us? 'Call no man father upon Earth', we are told: 'you have one Father in Heaven', a Father greater than Olympian Zeus, who can promise better things to those who overcome than the Elysian fields. The cares and corruptions of the world make it hard to re-member, hard to believe with real assent, what we are and what we are meant to be: but we are sons of the Living God, and he may call upon us to do great things. Much may be demanded of us; but in that case God will give us strength to meet the demand, if only we trust in him.

But suppose a man, through no fault of his own, finds himself confronted with a dilemma from which there is no honourable issue, or subjected to some pressure under which he cannot but choose evil? This can be envisaged as a possibility only by people who do not believe in God's Providence or do not think consequently about what such belief implies. A man who acts dishonourably, say in his married life, may indeed find himself in a situation where he cannot help wronging either A or B; but a man cannot get into such a dilemma innocently or by the fault of others. God does not require of a faithful servant the desperate choice between sin and sin.

Nor can a man's will be coerced into choosing evil; there is not, as propaganda of the enemy would have us believe, some scientific technique for such coercion that infallibly works. A tyrant may no doubt so abuse a man by drugs, sleeplessness, pain, sensory deprivation, and the like as to deprive him, temporarily or permanently, of the power of rational thought and choice; but that is not a victory over a man's will. It is a mere confusion to suppose that some technique could leave a man with the power of free choice and yet guarantee the way he chose; one might as well suppose that a superlative prestidigitator could succeed in thumb-catching.[1] If a man has a choice between alternatives, it is up to him which alternative is realized; we cannot consistently *both* suppose this to be so *and* believe that some technique of the tyrant's scientists guarantees the realization of one alternative before the victim chooses at all. So long as a choice is left, a brave choice is possible. Many men cracked in concentration camps; Maksymilian Kolbe triumphed.

What I have just said will provoke a two-fold attack: an attack on this kind of trust in Providence, and a depreciation of the courage induced by such trust. The

[1] I have found that not everybody knows what feat this word refers to. Insert your left thumb, pointing vertically upwards, into your clenched right hand, so that the tip of the tip of the thumb protrudes. Now move your left hand quickly round the top of your right hand, in time to catch hold of the tip of the thumb before it is pulled out! A lunatic, legend says, spent many hours trying to do this, but was never *quite* dexterous enough.

first attack would come not only from people who have no belief in God but also, I fear, from some professed Christians. To the first class of opponents I say for the present only this: think if you like that it is folly to believe in a God who will guide his children's steps so that they have not to choose between sin and sin; but in that case realize that you must abandon another criticism: that belief in God tells the believer nothing about what he may expect in the world, that it is irrefutable because vacuous.

The other class of opponents to this view of Providence are those who hold that a man leading an 'incarnational' life will identify himself with the world's concerns and plunge into its activities without care about keeping his hands clean. We have not so learned Christ, who was tempted in all points like us, yet without sin, and who fled to pray to his Father when men offered him an earthly kingdom. The Book of Daniel tells us, and daily observation confirms, that God gives the kingdoms of the world to the vilest of men; someone who covets earthly power may indeed find himself in an impasse with no decent way out. But we ought to pray, not that the rulers of the world may behave justly and love one another (for whatever the writers of bidding prayers may think, God has not promised to grant such petitions; quite the contrary) he has warned us that he will not bring about any such thing, but that the Kingdom may come, even in this our day.

Again, enemies of faith depreciate the courage of martyrs as compared with other men: those others were not expecting any blessing in an after-life, whereas the

martyrs died in confidence of a glorious heavenly reward. Such unbelievers fancy that a martyr's wishful thinking makes it all easy for him. But it is not after all so very easy to hang onto the faith that is the ground of such hope while enduring privations and tortures and the imminent danger of death. And the certainty faith affords is at best only a certainty that the great reward is attainable; not, that the man facing martyrdom will actually attain the reward.

More than one noble man has been assailed by temptation in the following form: suppose that before I die I should desperately wish for life even at the price of apostasy; and should therefore die unwillingly, and lose everything, here and hereafter? And we have records of how the temptation was faced. When St Thomas More's daughter put him the question: What if he should change his mind when it was too late to save his life? More replied: 'without my fault he will not let me be lost. I shall therefore with good hope commit myself wholly to him. And if he suffer me for my faults to perish, yet shall I serve for the praise of his justice.' Bunyan suffered the like temptation. The bullying justices who sentenced him to prison had threatened to send him from there to the gallows. Ignorant as he was of the law, he did not know whether this might not be his doom; and he had the chilling reflection that with the rope round his neck he might despair and be lost. And this is how he recorded his resolution.

> I am for going on and venturing my eternal state with Christ, whether I have comfort here or no. If God doth not come in, I thought, I will leap off the ladder even

blindfold into eternity, sink or swim, come Heaven, come
Hell. Lord Jesus, if thou wilt catch me, do; if not, I will
venture for thy name.

That is the courage of martyrs at its highest: an awesome
thing; let nobody dare to call it easy.

It is wrong, though common, to identify martyrdom
with dying for the truths of faith. All truth and justice
is God's truth and God's justice: a man does not cease to
be a martyr if the truth he dies for is not theological
truth, or the rights he dies defending are not the rights of
the Church. (Here I am at one with Aquinas: see
Summa Theologica, IIaIIae q.124 a.5.) A man would
be no less a martyr if a tyrant slew him for rebuking
injustice to the poor, or if a fundamentalist mob lynched
him for teaching that π is not 3, contrary to what 'it says
in the Bible' (3 Kings vii.23). If a man of faith dies for
truth and justice, he dies for God; and there must be
many people whose faith, as a new Canon of the Mass
says, is known to God alone.

Nevertheless we must maintain the old thesis that it is
not the death but the cause that makes the martyr. It
was not martyrdom when young 'idealistic' Germans
were killed in the early days of the Nazi movement:

Kameraden, die Rotfront und Reaktion erschossen.

Nor would it be martyrdom for an idolator to die in
defence of his idols, or for a fundamentalist to maintain
to the death against an infidel government that π *is*
equal to 3 because the Bible says so. As Aquinas puts it,
fidei non subest falsum. Faith that is known to God
alone still has to be faith in something true: faith is the

virtue by which a man can discern his genuine last end, from which he is disoriented by Original Sin, and can return to the true compass-bearing when temptations swerve him from it. And faith is only by the gift of God, who is Truth, who cannot set his seal upon a lie. The use of language by which false religions are called 'faiths' is grievously confusing; it is no virtue to believe unswervingly what is false, and one who dies for such belief does not die for faith and is no martyr.

This is one particular aspect of a general truth about courage: there can be no virtue in courage, in the facing of sudden danger or the endurance of affliction, if the cause for which this is done is worthless or positively vicious. Sometimes a dispute is raised on the issue whether we should say that such 'courage' is not really courage, or that it *is* courage but is not really a virtue. I do not think the issue is one of substance; since I introduced 'courage' as the name of a virtue, I shall keep to the former way of speaking, but nothing important hangs upon this. Endurance or defiance of danger in pursuance of a wrong end is not virtuous and in my book is not courageous either.

No courage, then, without the other moral virtues: in particular, no courage without prudence. The last dictum has a shade of paradox about it because the term 'prudence' has become devalued like other names of virtues, and has come to mean a shrewd regard for the safety of one's skin and worldly estate. The intended meaning is of course that there is no courage without a habit of sound judgment about practical situations. But in fact there are many situations in which the bravest

thing to do is actually the safest thing for the doer; though it may take a brave man to see this in an emergency. Alexander the Great, when a scaling-ladder broke behind him and he was left alone on top of the wall of a hostile city, immediately jumped down among the enemy; he was rescued by his men only after he had been grievously wounded; but if he had stayed on the wall, a target for spears and arrows, or had jumped back among his own men, he would certainly have perished.[1]

Conversely, any ascription of virtue other than courage may be defeated if a lack of courage is established. The Polish judge in *Ashes and Diamonds* might have been regarded as a virtuous citizen if he had died before the war or in the Resistance: his yielding to be a creature of the Germans when he was in the concentration camp, beating and torturing his fellow prisoners to save his own skin – and perhaps even more, his plea when finally exposed that this unhappy episode of an abnormal time should be buried in oblivion and he return to a civil career that could still be useful and honourable – clearly shows that his previous adherence to virtuous ways was only provisional, so long as things did not get too tough, and therefore was not virtue at all. Such reflections should make us tremble for ourselves, but not despair; God will not let his friends be tempted beyond their strength; and we are to be judged only according to our works, not according to the way God knows we would have behaved in circumstances that never arose.

[1] It is amusing that Hume rejects such stories of Alexander's valour as contrary to all human experience; of course *he* had never met a general who would act like that!

(The very ascription of such hypothetical knowledge to God is dubious, because it is doubtful whether there is such a thing as the way a man *definitely would* have acted, to be picked out from the various ways he *might* have acted.)

Courage, then, cannot exist apart from some virtue other than courage, whose exercise sometimes calls for courage; conversely, the exercise of another virtue may always call for courage, the world being what it is, so no virtue can exist in due development without courage. This raises the general question of the so-called unity of the virtues. There can obviously be no question of a unity of the various human vices; vices are various and often mutually incompatible. But the virtues are all at least mutually compatible; and our nature is not so radically flawed that progress in one virtue necessarily carries with it deterioration in respect of another. The question now is whether the virtues all entail one another. In considering this question, I shall begin by leaving out of account the theological virtues, when using such expressions as '(all) the virtues'.

There is a classic argument to show that the virtues do all entail one another, which I shall come to presently. If this argument were valid, and based on true premises, it would lead to a grimmer view of human nature than we have so far seen reason to hold: it would mean that if a man is manifestly affected with one vice, then any virtue that he may seem to have along with his vice is only spurious, and really he is vicious in this respect too and not entitled to the admiration that his virtue seems to call for. Of course it is nowise an argument against a

thesis that if true it exposes to sight some very grim
aspect of human life that is not commonly realized; and
it is no *decisive* counter-argument that the thing is contrary to ordinary human moral judgments. (The view that
there is no moral prescription that may not be violated
in extreme circumstances probably forms part of ordinary
human moral judgment; but I have argued that it is
certainly false.) But it would need an extremely cogent
argument to overthrow the apparent teaching of human
experience all the world over that a man may be very
laudable in some respects and very faulty in others. And
I shall try to show that no such cogent argument is
forthcoming, and that therefore the thesis of the unity
of the virtues must be rejected as false. We may thank
God that it is false; the world would present a very
terrible aspect if we had to think that anyone who is
morally faulty by reason of one habitual grave defect
must be totally devoid of virtue; that any virtues such
faulty people seem to have are worthless shams.

The devastating consequences of holding the unity of
the virtues are often disguised from people because they
have an excessively narrow conception of moral virtue. It
is of course notorious that a man may work skilfully and
devotedly at some art, science, or public office and yet
be in some respect grossly vicious; like Harry Graham's
organist, who

> starves his children, beats his wife . . .
> But dash it all, what can you say?
> You haven't heard the beggar play!

But many people hold ethical views according to which

the labours of the artist or scientist require and evince no moral virtue at all — perhaps they would judge the statesman or civil servant differently — and then they fail to see that such cases are on the face of it evidence against the unity of the virtues. Perhaps this darkness can be dispelled at once by clear exposition: it scarcely needs argument to establish the preposterousness of a view by which a man needs no moral virtue at all to work well in the main and worthy task of his life.

The classic argument for the unity of the virtues proceeds by seeking to show that loss or lack of any one virtue carries with it loss or lack of all the others. If you lack any moral, behavioural, virtue, then your judgment of what is to be done will be corrupted; for the habit of sound moral judgment, the virtue of prudence, is not to be gained just by learning lessons from some lecturer or textbook on moral philosophy or moral theology; it has to be gained and reinforced in practice in dealing with your own actual situation; so corrupt habits of action in any area will destroy the habit of prudence. But no behavioural virtue is a virtue at all unless behaviour is regulated by prudent judgments. So loss of any one behavioural virtue is ruinous to prudence, and thereby to any other behavioural virtue. No prudence, then, if any one behavioural virtue is lacking; if prudence is lacking, no behavioural virtue is still a virtue; so all the virtues stand or fall together.

The conclusion is, I have said, both odious and preposterous; and it is easy to detect the flaw in the reasoning. There is a tacit assumption that if a man's habit of sound moral judgment is vitiated anywhere

it is vitiated everywhere. This would follow only if men formed their judgments with rigorous consistency; but notoriously they do nothing of the kind, and we may thank God that they do not. The main line of thought they are on may lead to Hell, but providentially they are shunted off onto a side-line. Aquinas followed the view I am arguing to be wrong when he treated of the unity of the virtues; but he saw the point I am making about consistency when he discussed the virtue of faith. No false judgment can come from, still less constitute, an exercise of the virtue of faith; but this does not mean that a false judgment destroys faith in a man because its logical consequences would do so if he accepted them; as, given human inconsistency, he very often will not. If a man's habit of sound moral judgment is vitiated anywhere, then it is *at risk* everywhere; but not all dangers issue in disasters.

It may be surprising that a Professor of Logic should thank God for human inconsistency. Let us however consider briefly from a logical point of view what is the evil of inconsistency. When our thought floats free from contact with reality, inconsistency matters little or not at all. Inconsistency in a fictional narrative matters only if it upsets the reader; if it emerges only upon careful consideration and the readers are not shocked in fact, then it were vain for a critic to say they ought to have been. Again, if the rules of a game, say chess, are imperfectly formulated, so that in some *outré* position there are incompatible prescriptions as to which moves are now lawful, this does not so to say vitiate all the chess that has hitherto been played. Whether a moral can be drawn

from this about inconsistencies in mathematical deductive systems that emerge by some complicated deductions is a question for the philosophy of mathematics.

Inconsistency matters precisely where *judging* inconsistently is involved: to judge inconsistently involves judging wrongly. An inconsistent factual narrative will at some point be factually false; an inconsistent set of instructions will in some detail be unexecutable; an inconsistent moral code will on some matter be morally objectionable. This is the evil of inconsistency: this, and this only. A man who falls into inconsistency does not incur the further evil of a special sort of wrongness, logical wrongness; it is only that logic suffices to show that somewhere or other (logic does not say where) he is wrong in a non-logical way.

This may be brought out clearly by considering the so-called Paradox of the Preface. A's preface says that A's book no doubt still contains errors, for which the kind friends who have helped him to remove other errors are not responsible; B's preface says that though kind friends have tried to persuade him that some things he said are wrong, he stands by everything he has written. We should judge A to be a man of good sense, B to be a conceited ass; yet A's preface ensures that the total corpus of A's book – preface *plus* text – is inconsistent, and B's does not ensure anything of the sort about B's corpus. Is it then wise to be inconsistent, foolish to be consistent? People puzzle themselves about this only because they have (at least at the back of their minds) the idea of inconsistency as a specially virulent sort of error.

But our relative estimate of the two prefaces is in fact simply explained. Given human fallibility, the text without the preface will in fact contain errors both in A's book and in B's: A incurs no further error, let alone a worse sort of error, by recognizing this; B aggravates his errors by saying there are none to be found.

We are liable to inconsistency as we are liable to error, and we should not acquiesce in gross and remediable inconsistency; but A incurred a charge of inconsistency only because he acknowledged that he must have made undetected errors; and he was not more worthy of censure for this confession. Being inconsistent implies having gone astray; but not all error, all wrong judgment, is equally bad, and inconsistency in the right place may save a man from worse errors than if he were not there inconsistent. This is the way that Providence uses one kind of human failing to mitigate or prevent a worse one.

In Hume's *Dialogues on Natural Religion* his mouth-piece Philo arraigns God's Providence for the prevalence of laziness. But given that God gives rein to other human vices, it is well that men are lazy: as also that they are incompetent and prone to take bribes. How much more affliction tyrants would cause if their minions were sea-green incorruptibles, flawlessly efficient and indefatigably industrious! Nor is it only for the sake of his fellows that the bad man's worst vices are partly neutralized by his laziness, incompetence, and venality; in his own soul too these minor vices may prevent his major vices from coming to full development and obliterating what of good is left in him.

So far, then, from accepting the doctrine of unity of the

virtues, I hold that two vices may be better than one, or at any rate less bad, even for the man's own condition. But after all what good is such imperfect virtue? Is it not really spurious virtue? Not necessarily. With Aquinas (*Summa Theologica*, IIaIIae q.47 a.13) I hold that we must distinguish between a man who pursues good ends and a man who pursues bad or worthless ends. Take the case of a man set on financial gain; he may plan cleverly and farsightedly, boldly confront dangers, say in exploration of possibly valuable rock strata, and abstain from distracting short-term enjoyment and sexual entanglements; but he has not then the virtues of prudence, courage, temperance, and chastity; nor has he the virtue of justice if his word is his bond because he shrewdly calculates that honesty is the best policy. But that is no reason for rejecting as spurious the virtues, say, of an old Roman who made the good of the Republic the main goal of his life.

All virtues, however, are in the end vain for a man without the theological virtues of faith, hope and charity. Without these a man cannot attain his last end; without faith he cannot even see how to orient himself towards it. Without hope he will lose the way through presumptuous neglect of dangers, or lie down and perish from despair. And the taste for the music of Heaven is an acquired one; unless it is acquired here, by the practice of charity, a man is in such a state that those heavenly harmonies could only be torment to him.

Only by the theological virtues can a man overcome that deadly drift of his nature in the wrong direction which Christians call Original Sin. Without them he

may for a time avoid gross misdeeds, but not permanently, because he cannot always be so vigilant (cf.
Summa Theologica, IaIIae q.109 a.8). Because *each* sin
was avoidable, a man devoid of grace and theological
virtues is still acting with free choice and answerable
for what he does; because *not all* are avoidable, he is a
slave to sin. (This is no contradiction: just as one might
say without contradiction of an overloaded boat that
although *each* passenger could stay in it without its
sinking, *not all* can do so.)

Without charity, the non-theological virtues may be
genuine, though limited, goods. On the other hand
charity is incompatible with any gross defect in these
virtues. Such gross defect would mean a failure in
charity too: for nobody thus faulty could meet the
criterion for charity that I cited earlier from Aquinas;
an attachment to God so great that sooner than be
separated from him one would lose any other good or
suffer any evil.

What of the connexion between the theological virtues
themselves? The Catholic tradition is that that faith
which is a gift of God can exist even if for a time a
man lapses from charity. Faith without charity is like
a tree that has been cut down to the roots: it will bear
no fruit, and if it does not send out a new shoot even
the root may die, but so long as the root lives there is
still hope of revival. Or again, one may say that a man
who has faith but has lost charity is like a mariner driven
off course who still has his compass; if the compass too
had gone overboard, the chance of final shipwreck would
be greatly increased. But the chance that faith will revive

into the flowers and fruits of charity is slender unless hope is left as well as faith. The old saying 'Honour lost, much lost; hope lost, all lost' is not quite true, but the case of a man who has lost the virtue of hope, whether by despair or presumption, is very grievous: traditionally, despair and presumption are 'sins against the Holy Ghost', by which a man not only falls from grace but puts the greatest obstacles to any recovery from the fall.

Charity, love, is what men are for, and without gaining this they have lost everything. In this book I have often cited McTaggart, to whom I owe so much in my thought; I shall end with the words with which he ended *The Nature of Existence*.

> Of the nature of that good we know something. We know that it is a timeless and endless state of love – love so direct, so intimate, and so powerful that even the deepest mystic rapture gives us but the slightest foretaste of its perfection. We know that we shall know nothing but our beloved, and those they love, and ourselves as loving them, and that only in this shall we seek and find satisfaction. Between the present and that fruition there stretches a future which may well need courage. For, while there will be in it much good, and increasing good, there may await us evils which we can now measure only by their infinite insignificance as compared with the final reward.

INDEX OF PROPER NAMES